ESSAYS
ON
POLITICAL ORGANIZATION,

SELECTED FROM AMONG THOSE SUBMITTED IN COMPETITION
FOR THE PRIZES OFFERED BY THE

UNION LEAGUE
OF
PHILADELPHIA.

PHILADELPHIA:
COLLINS, PRINTER, 705 JAYNE STREET.
1868.

Union League House,

MAY 15, 1867.

AT a meeting of the Board of Directors of the UNION LEAGUE OF PHILADELPHIA, held March 12th, 1867, the following preamble and resolutions were adopted:—

WHEREAS, In a republican form of government it is of the highest importance that the delegates of the people, to whom the sovereign power is intrusted, should be so selected as to truly represent the body politic, and there being no provision of law whereby the people may be organized for the purpose of such selection, and all parties having recognized the necessity of such organization, by the formation of voluntary associations for this purpose: and

WHEREAS, There are grave defects existing under the present system of voluntary organization, which it is believed may be corrected by suitable provisions of law: Now, therefore, be it

Resolved, By the Board of Directors of the UNION LEAGUE OF PHILADELPHIA, that the Secretary be, and is hereby, directed to offer eleven hundred dollars in prizes for essays on the legal organization of the people to select candidates for office, the prizes to be as follows, viz:—

The sum of five hundred dollars for that essay which, in the judgment of the Board, shall be first in the order of merit;
Three hundred dollars for the second;
Two hundred dollars for the third; and
One hundred for the fourth.

The conditions upon which these prizes are offered are as follows, viz:—

First. All essays competing for these prizes must be addressed to GEORGE H. BOKER, Secretary of the UNION LEAGUE OF PHILADELPHIA, and must be received by him before the first day of January, 1868; and no communication having the author's name attached, or with any other indication of origin, will be considered.

Second. Accompanying every competing essay, the author must inclose his name and address within a sealed envelope, addressed to the Secretary of the UNION LEAGUE. After the awards have been made, the envelopes accompanying the successful essays shall be opened, and the authors notified of the result.

Third. All competing essays shall become the property of the UNION LEAGUE; but no publication of rejected essays, or the name of their authors, shall be made without consent of the authors in writing.

By order of the Board of Directors.

GEO. H. BOKER,
Secretary.

A PLAN

BY WHICH

POLITICAL PARTIES IN A REPUBLIC

MAY BE

LEGALLY EMPOWERED TO SELECT CANDIDATES FOR OFFICE.

BY

W. E. BARBER,
WEST CHESTER, PA.

A PLAN

BY WHICH

POLITICAL PARTIES IN A REPUBLIC MAY BE LEGALLY EMPOWERED TO SELECT CANDIDATES FOR OFFICE.

The assumption that the people are the fountain of all political power, is the corner-stone of the American Republic.

In the language of Webster in his reply to Hayne, "It is the people's constitution, the people's government, made for the people, made by the people, and answerable to the people." The will of the majority, clearly and fairly expressed, is the inexorable rule to which the nation has submitted for nearly a century. It controls all elections held by the citizens; it sways all assemblages of the people, whether primary, or representative in their character; and is emphatically the "higher law" of the land. Where its voice is distinctly heard, there is no alternative but prompt obedience. Only when it utters an "uncertain sound," is there any profit in gainsaying, or pretext for delay.

If, however, the subject-matter with regard to which the people have pronounced their decision, has not been properly, or intelligibly, presented for their consideration, or if the qualified citizens have been subjected to any kind of *duress*, amounting to a denial of freedom of action, or opinion, then a preponderance of votes in any direction is not a true expression of the will of the majority. In such cases, whilst all good citizens will bow, submissively for the time, to the popular edict, it is their right and duty to devise and suggest the means by which such errors of the popular judgment may, in the future, be avoided.

It has long been a question in the minds of thoughtful men of every party in this country, whether the system under which party nominations for office are usually effected, is not radically unfair, and subversive of the principles which lie at the foundation of our republican institutions.

In too many instances, the party ticket is moulded by the hands of a few active, determined, and unprincipled political managers, in the interest of persistent office-seekers in each election district; whilst the body of citizens constituting the organization of which this active minority is only a small fraction, is expected to ratify, without questioning, the nominations thus fabricated for their suffrages. Hence, individuals utterly unfitted by reason of ignorance, inexperience, repulsive habits, and depraved moral character, constantly mount into positions of emolument and power, through the instrumentality of reputable citizens, who abhor the nominations, and silently protest against the necessity, which, as they conceive, constrains them to support incompetent and obnoxious candidates.

Occasionally there are found men, upon whom party obligations sit lightly, who prefer to sacrifice their right of suffrage rather than sustain objectionable nominees. The number of such independent citizens generally increases with the growing strength of the political organization to which they are attached; for, in proportion to the augmentation of the power of a party, corrupt men become bolder in their determination to secure their nominations, and conscientious citizens grow more and more dissatisfied with tickets framed out of such contaminated materials, until, finally, they abandon the organization whose principles they fully indorse, and would, if they could, cheerfully sustain.

Defections of this character are often erroneously attributed to apathy and indifference, and frequently cause the overthrow of a strong party at the very zenith of its supremacy. But the inquiry may be suggested whether the grievances of which these good citizens complain are not the natural result of their own dereliction. Is it not the manifest duty of every elector who regards the right of suffrage as a precious privilege, to attend the primary meetings of the party, and so impress the weight of his character and influence upon the proceedings, as to secure the selection of honorable and upright men to represent the district in the nominating conventions? In these elementary assemblages of the people lie all the plastic materials out of which the ticket is subsequently fashioned. Here the power is generated which propels all the party machinery. Here, if anywhere, the will of the majority ought to be clearly manifested. What extenuation can be offered sufficient to justify good citizens in their refusal to participate in these formative assemblies; and with what consistency can they, after allowing improper nominations to be made through their default, complain of the results of their own inaction?

In answer to this arraignment, many of our most substantial fellow-citizens would declare that they recognize no obligation of citizenship which would require them to take part in these meetings as they are usually conducted. How can it be expected, they would say, that sober, industrious, self-respecting, and God-fearing men should leave their shops, their counting-houses, their factories, and their farms, and periodically repair to the party "Head-Quarters," redolent of noisome odors, and reeking with the ribaldry and blasphemies of excessive stimulation, and spend their valuable time in fruitless endeavors to obtain a proper representation of their wishes and sentiments!

They generally find that the delegates to represent the district in the convention, have been indicated, previous to the organization of the meeting, by a caucus of astute manipulators, and that no option is left to the quiet citizen except to support the individuals designated, which is a work of supererogation, or to undertake the hopeless task of defeating the caucus nominees. If a candidate for any one of the offices, however unimportant, should happen to be a resident of the election district, it would be considered an act of the highest discourtesy to him to *instruct* the delegates: they are, by common consent and immemorial usage, deemed to be *his* delegates, subject to be bartered, sold, or exchanged, like cattle in the market; bound to secure his nomination by the use of all the artifices, honorable or otherwise, known to politicians, even at the sacrifice of every other interest involved in the canvass.

If by a rare accident there should be no resident candidate, all the instructions that may be imposed upon the delegates are powerless, in most cases, to hold them to their obligations to their constituents; for, by the time they have reached the convention, they have lost all their political virtue and their moral integrity, and often shamelessly foist upon the party a batch of nominations evidently purchased and paid for in money, or with promises of reciprocal influence, or pledges of place, on the part of the successful nominees.

That the picture is not overdrawn, is within the knowledge of almost every intelligent elector who has ever participated in primary meetings, or closely observed the proceedings of political conventions.

Is there, then, no remedy for these evils with which the body politic is afflicted? Is there no alternative but a hopeless surrender of the dearest of our political rights to the machinations of designing and corrupt politicians?

Fortunately no such necessity exists. There is a remedy, sure, simple, and easy of application. But it involves the utter extirpation of the morbid gland which deranges the functions of our political system. Party nominations for office will never be pure, fair, or satisfactory, *until delegate conventions are entirely abolished.* Candidates must be confronted with the people, without the intervention of intriguing middle-men, in order that the ends aimed at by the Fathers in establishing our institutions shall be accomplished; or, in the words of the lamented Lincoln, "that the nation shall, under God, have a new birth of freedom, and that the government of the people, by the people, and for the people, shall not perish from the earth." Men must be elevated to office, not because they have the means of purchasing their nominations, but because they are *honest;* not because they possess a circumscribed ward, or township, popularity, but because they are *capable;* not because they make loud professions and proffer high-sounding guarantees of their purposes in the future, when safely in the enjoyment of office, but because they have well-established reputations for fidelity, in the past, to all their duties and engagements as citizens. Of qualifications such as these, the people are more competent judges than are delegate conventions.

When our nominating system shall have been purified of this offensive feature, the power must be wrested from the hands of the petty oligarchies, which have, from time immemorial, controlled the primary meetings. For this purpose, *legislation* is absolutely essential. The safeguards required to enable the people freely to select, from among the numerous candidates, such only as are most worthy to fill the offices in their gift, cannot be secured by means of voluntary associations. Some legal tribunal is imperatively demanded, before which questions as to the qualifications of voters at primary elections may be authoritatively settled. In this, as in other respects, what is known as the "Crawford County System" is fatally defective. It does not reach the seat of the disease, and therefore falls short of the efficiency claimed for it by its advocates. It is destitute of the legal sanctions and inquisitorial power essential to the purity of elections. It provides no mode by which a party, attempting to indicate its choice of candidates, may be protected from the intrusion, on the one hand, of persons who are not qualified citizens under existing laws, and, on the other hand, from the interference of men of contrary political sentiments. Besides, the officers of primary elections under that system, are generally chosen in great haste, just before the opening of the polls, and are under no obligations, except such as are common to all citizens, to discharge their duties faithfully; and as their term of office expires with the enumeration of the votes cast at the election, it is impossible to hold them to a strict accountability for any delinquencies they may commit. That these officers ought always to act under the sanction of an oath, is apparent from the consideration, that nominations made by the dominant party of a county, or city, are usually equivalent to the election of the nominees.

It is proposed, therefore, to establish, *by law*, a mode of organization to be adopted by any political party in this State, which, upon being accepted, shall be obligatory in all its details. The general outlines of the proposed system, the particulars of which are set forth in the bill hereto appended, may be briefly described, as follows, viz:—

All nominations heretofore made by city and county conventions, to be hereafter made by the recognized members of each party at primary elections.

An Executive, or Managing Committee, for each city or county, to be constituted by the election of one member of said committee for each ward, or township, at its annual primary election, which Executive Committee shall have the superintendence and direction of the party canvass in such city or county, until its successor shall be pronounced duly elected.

This Executive Committee shall annually appoint a Judge and two Inspectors of Primary Elections for each ward or township within the limits of its jurisdiction, and shall designate the place in each election district at which such elections shall be held—the time to be fixed by law.

These election officers shall be sworn, or affirmed, to discharge their duties faithfully, and shall exercise the same powers and be liable to the same penalties for misdemeanors, as are provided by law for officers of general elections in the commonwealth.

The Executive Committee shall furnish to the election officers of each district a certified list of citizens who voted at the next preceding general election in such district. This can always be procured from the prothonotary of each county.

No person shall be permitted to vote at such primary election, whose name is not found on the list of voters at the preceding general election, and who shall not be able to satisfy the election officers, if his vote be challenged, by the testimony under oath of at least one qualified citizen in good standing in the party, as well as by his own oath, that he voted the ticket of the party at the next preceding general election: Provided, that recognized members of the party who were necessarily absent from the preceding general election, and minors who will become of age at or before the next ensuing general election, and who shall publicly announce their intention to support the ticket to be nominated by the party holding said primary election, shall be entitled to vote notwithstanding their names shall not be found on said list of voters.

At the close of the election, the member of the Executive Committee who shall be in office at the time of said primary election, shall take charge of the ballot-boxes, election papers, and one of the certificates of election for each office voted for (another of said certificates for each office to be sent by mail to the Chairman of the acting Executive Committee) in the ward, or township, represented by him, and shall produce them at the county seat within a specified time, at a meeting of all the members of the Acting Executive Committee, who shall then be severally sworn, or affirmed, to discharge the duties of return judges; and having ascertained the names of the candidates receiving the highest number of votes for each office voted for, shall make and sign returns, which shall be delivered to the Chairman of the Executive Committee elect. In case of a tie vote for any two or more candidates for the same office, the Committee shall decide by ballot which of said candidates shall receive the nomination.

With the performance of these duties the term of office of the Acting Executive Committee will have expired.

The newly elected members of the Executive Committee shall assemble at the county seat, at a time to be designated, and having organized by the election of a chairman and secretary, shall open the returns and publish the names of the candidates nominated for the several offices, in the organs of the party. A short time previous to the Primary Election, they should issue a circular containing the names of the candidates for the several offices to be voted for, and the time and place of holding the Primary Elections in each ward and township; and, if deemed advisable, a brief explanation of the system might be appended, and a short appeal to the members of the party to attend the elections and manifest their choice of candidates. These circulars can be placed in the hands of every party voter, through the instrumentality of Vigilance Committees for each ward and township, to be appointed by the Executive Committee.

Personal solicitation for influence and support, on the part of candidates, should be discountenanced by every means possible, and the people should be permitted to express their sentiments with the utmost freedom.

It is claimed that under this proposed system, a Registry of party voters will not be necessary; that the practice of office-seeking will be measurably broken up; and that positions of honor and profit will be conferred, as a rule, upon the capable and deserving.

No provision is made by the proposed legislation for the remuneration of the election officers, and of the members of the Executive Committee when acting as Return Judges. Some compensation will probably be necessary to secure their attendance, but it had better be regulated by each party for itself. The necessary funds for this purpose could readily be obtained by assessing the nominated candidates in proportion to the value of the several offices, and by an understanding, that each citizen should make a small contribution towards such expenses, when he deposits his vote at the Primary Elections.

AN ACT

Relating to the Selection of Candidates for Office by Political Parties in this Commonwealth.

SEC. 1. *Be it enacted, etc.* That it shall be lawful for qualified citizens constituting any political party in this commonwealth to adopt the following system of organization, viz:—

SEC. 2. The Acting Executive Committee of any such party, in any county, or any city of this commonwealth, is hereby authorized, on or before the first day of July succeeding the passage of this act, to appoint from the qualified citizens of said party, one Judge and two Inspectors in each ward, or township, of said county, or city, who shall conduct the Primary, or Nominating Elections of said party, in the manner hereinafter directed.

SEC. 3. The Executive Committee before-mentioned shall procure, from the prothonotary of said county, a certified copy of the list of citizens who voted at each election district in said county at the last previous general election, and shall transmit the same to one of the election officers appointed in each of said districts as aforesaid, at least one week previous to said Primary or Nominating Election.

SEC. 4. Each of the Inspectors, appointed as aforesaid, shall appoint one Clerk, and each Judge, Inspector, and Clerk aforesaid, before entering upon the duties of their offices respectively, shall take and subscribe the oath prescribed to be taken by the officers of general elections under the laws of this commonwealth.

SEC. 5. The qualified voters of said party shall meet in the several wards, or townships, of each of said counties and cities, at such place as shall be designated by said Acting Executive Committee, on the   Tuesday of August, next after the passage of this act, and then and there elect, by ballot, one member of the Executive Committee of the party, in each of said counties and cities, to represent each of said wards and townships, and they shall, in the same manner, designate and select the names of such candidates for the offices to be voted for at the next ensuing general election, as they may desire to be nominated for the said offices.

Sec. 6. Every such Nominating Election shall be opened at twelve o'clock, meridian, and shall be closed at six o'clock in the evening of said day.

Sec. 7. Every Inspector, or Judge, appointed as aforesaid, shall have power to administer oaths, or affirmations, to any and all persons claiming a right to vote at said Primary, or Nominating Election, and shall be subject to all such penalties for misdemeanors in office, as are prescribed for the officers of general elections held under the laws of this commonwealth.

Sec. 8. No person shall be permitted to vote at such Primary, or Nominating Election, who is not a qualified citizen under the laws of this commonwealth; and unless his name is found on the list of citizens who voted in said ward, or township, at the last preceding general election, furnished by the Executive Committee as aforesaid; and unless, further, such person shall have voted at such general election for the candidates nominated by the party holding such Primary Election; and if the right of any person to vote is objected to for the reason that he is not a member of the party holding said Primary Election, it shall be the duty of the Inspectors to examine such person on oath or affirmation, and the fact that he voted for the nominees of said party at the previous general election shall be substantiated, in addition to his own oath or affirmation, by the testimony of at least one qualified citizen in good standing in said party. Provided, that recognized members of the party who were absent from the district at the last general election, and whose vote is not objected to, may vote, although his name is not found on the list of voters aforesaid; and provided, further, that persons who are under the age of twenty-one years, but who will arrive at said age on or before the next ensuing general election, shall be entitled to vote upon making public declaration of their intention to vote, at the next general election, for the candidates nominated by the party holding such Primary Election.

Sec. 9. When the polls shall be closed, the tickets shall be counted in the same manner as is prescribed by law for the enumeration of tickets voted at the general elections.

Sec. 10. As soon as the votes given for any office are counted, public announcement shall be made by the Judge of the election, of the number of votes cast for each person voted for; and the officers of the election shall make out two certificates under their hands, setting forth the number of votes cast for the several persons voted for, and shall deliver one of said certificates to the acting member of the Executive Committee in said ward or township, and shall transmit the other of said certificates by mail to the Chairman of the Executive Committee then in office.

SEC. 11. After the election is finished, the tickets, lists of voters, tally papers, and forms of oath subscribed by the election officers, shall be placed in an envelope which shall be bound with tape and sealed by the election officers, and delivered to the member of the Executive Committee representing the district in which the said Primary Election has been held.

SEC. 12. On the following Tuesday after the election, the members of the Acting Executive Committee representing the several wards or townships in any county or city, shall assemble at the county seat of the several counties, at the usual place of meeting of said committee, and shall then be sworn, or affirmed, by the nearest justice of the peace, to discharge their duties as Return Judges; and shall proceed to add together the number of votes appearing by the certificates aforesaid to have been given for any person or persons in respect to any office, and after ascertaining the number of such votes shall make out and sign returns, which shall be delivered by the chairman of said committee to the person who shall be subsequently elected chairman of the newly elected Executive Committee: Provided, that in case of a tie vote given to any two or more persons for the same office, the said committee, acting as Return Judges, shall vote by ballot, and the person having the highest number of votes of said committee, shall be declared nominated for said office.

SEC. 13. The newly elected members of the Executive Committee for each of said counties and cities, shall assemble on the following ———, and shall organize by the selection, by ballot, of a Chairman and Secretary. They shall then open the returns delivered to the Chairman, by the retiring Executive Committee, and shall cause publication of the candidates, nominated for the several offices, to be made in the party papers of the city or county.

SECT. 14. The Executive Committee for each county and city elected as aforesaid, shall, in every year hereafter, perform the duties hereinbefore prescribed to be done by the Acting Committee in office at the passage of this act.

LEGAL

NOMINATIONS.

BY
CHAS. G. CAME,
JOURNAL OFFICE, BOSTON.

LEGAL NOMINATIONS.

THE CAUCUS SYSTEM.

The caucus system, as for the sake of simplicity we shall designate the general method of making nominations hitherto prevalent in the United States, is so well understood that we need give no further account of it than is necessary to get a clear idea of its defects. Not but that it has great merits. They are such as not only to account for its long-continued sway in this country, but to inspire the prediction that wherever in the world republican institutions are introduced, they will carry with them this disciplinary and almost coordinate rule of "King Caucus." But among us the system has become so overlaid and tainted with abuses, that we meet on every hand the inquiry, whether it is not possible to supplant it with something which, with at least equal efficiency, shall give us better results.

HOW IT IS MADE TO WORK.

For the purpose of exhibiting some of the more ordinary working evils of the caucus system, let us give a brief illustration drawn from the experience of thousands: An honest member of one of our great political organizations goes to a primary meeting called for the selection of candidates for office. He has his own ideas, if not of the proper persons to be nominated, yet of the proper class from which they should be taken. Perhaps he finds the majority present well disposed in the same direction; perhaps he finds an honest disagreement which might easily be reconciled under favorable circumstances. But he soon finds, also, a knot of men, having a perfect understanding with each other, working with great assiduity and skill for other aspirants, who, we will say, are positively unworthy, if not disreputable. The unwary and indifferent are wheedled, the mercenary bought up, the timid overawed, misrepresentations set afloat and dissensions inflamed, and, in short, a resort is had to the whole stock of expedients "in such cases made and provided," until either a majority outright is secured or such a commanding plurality as can make its own terms. And how then is the honest dissentient, profoundly impressed with the unfitness of the nomination, and the reckless means by which it was brought about, to help himself? If he calls another caucus, which, of course, he has no right to do, the same result would probably be repeated. Shall he bolt? If so, he either throws away his vote, which his party may ill afford to lose, or he votes for the opposition candidates, which is a stab at his own avowed principles. In either case his standing with his party colleagues suffers, and he sets a precedent which his victors of to-day might follow to his own grief to-morrow. It is true that instances do occur where nominations so bad, and accomplished by such outrageous methods, are made, that it is a man's duty to deliberately refuse them his support, no matter what may be the consequence at the polls. But these extreme cases are so rare that, like the right of revolution, they may be left to take care of themselves. The usual course will always be to submit to a result which, stated in its mildest form, is the government of the community by the minority of a party

ANALYSIS OF ITS EVILS.

An analysis even of this imperfect illustration will show that the evils of the caucus system are resolvable into two classes: Packing, and what, for want of a better general name, we shall call the Perturbations of the moment. The first—which may be defined an attempt to control a meeting through a force of interested men—is the prime, peculiar, and prolific evil of the caucus system. To pack a caucus has been the study of three generations of American politicians, and it is not surprising that the result is the perfection of art, high or low, according as reference is had either to skill or to morality. The simplest method is to get together a numerical majority of the caucus to accomplish an effect contrary to the wishes of a majority of the political organization concerned. It may be done merely by the superior vigilance arising from personal interest over the disinterestedness of the masses of the party; or it may be secured by bribery or any other reprehensible means. But a well-packed minority often answers every purpose of its directors. Its complete understanding and unity of action are decisive in the midst of division, indecision, and indifference. It is in vain for the few who detect the plotting to foil it by ordinary methods. Suppose, in order to avoid a ballot under such disadvantages, a marking list is opened—the packers are the first to concentrate their strength where it tells on every subsequent man whose choice is not fixed, or who is willing to fall in with the apparent majority, or whose chief desire is to settle the matter and go home. Or again, an aroused member of the meeting thinks he sees a chance of defeating the wire-pullers, and he moves that the nominations be made by a committee. Very well, how shall this committee be raised? By the chair. The chair is already packed, and the pockets of the incumbent are likewise packed with a select list of committee men. In cases where there are to be several nominees, the packers may be interested only in a portion of the names, but these may be so mixed with those of an unexceptionable character that the caucus is often coerced into taking the bad, in order to avoid losing the good.

The second class of evils, grouped as perturbations of the moment, comprises all those influences which affect men in crowds against the calm conclusions of their individual judgment. They do not necessarily imply fraud, but possibly indiscreet effort on one side, and credulity or indifference or weakness on the other. Instances like the last mentioned may sometimes be classed under this head; for it not unfrequently happens that the alternative of voting for candidates whom we do not desire in order to save those whom we do prefer is forced on us by those who are as well intentioned as ourselves, and who, also, may sacrifice their preferences to quite as great an extent in accepting our favorites. Hence comes the best form of what is known as "log-rolling"—the "I will suit you on the ticket, if you will suit me"—the result being that nobody is exactly suited. This springs from the direct temptation toward bargaining held out by the caucus system. Other frequent means of biasing an honest judgment are the prestige or exertions of influential persons; a speech or a joke, telling for the moment and for the moment only; the tendency to go with the majority, even upon the strength of indications as to its direction which are accidental or deceptive; in short, the thousand and one misleading influences resulting from the action of men in bodies, as distinguished from the exercise of their cool judgment individually.

That which is sometimes spoken of as the crowning evil of the caucus system, namely, the binding authority of its action, is nothing of the kind. This obligation, indeed, must constitute the final efficiency of any system, and it only works wrongfully when it is made to give effect to antecedent abuses.

AN OBJECTION IN ADVANCE.

Such, in brief, are the more obvious evils of the prevalent system of making political nominations. The cry for reform is general and urgent. But when we come to look in that direction, we are apt to encounter a suggestion which, at first, wears a formidable appearance. We are told that the caucus system works well enough in practice wherever the best men of a party are in the habit of attending the primary meetings in any fair proportion to their numbers; but, as they generally do not so attend, and will not, it is hardly worth while to seek for any mere change of methods. In reply, it is to be said that, to a certain extent, the objection is irrelevant, for this indifference of otherwise good men to political duties is often owing to causes quite beyond the sphere of our inquiry, and calls for remedies in their nature moral and educational. The problem which we are now discussing is, how to take our communities, with all their indifference, and just as we find them, and thence educe the best possible nominations. But, secondly, this suggestion, instead of being an objection to reformatory efforts, is, when at all applicable, the strongest argument in their favor; for it is undeniable that much of this standing aloof of the best men of all parties is due directly to the humiliating machinations of caucuses, which prevent them from having their just weight in council, improperly neutralize their votes, and too often subject them to personal indignities. The importance of this point is too obvious to need any elaboration

PLAN PROPOSED.

Uniform experience since the foundation of our Government has shown that all political action has been, and is ever likely to be, carried on through the agency of great parties, but two of which generally exist at a time, whose modes of operation, especially in the nomination of candidates, are substantially the same. To elements so simple and constant as these there would seem to be no difficulty in applying the regulating efficiency and the sanction of law. The plan of accomplishing this, which we venture to propose, although it is susceptible of modifications in every part, may be outlined as follows:—

In all cases let the State make provision for an accurate registry list. At a specified time previous to any election at which candi dates are to be voted for, let the list be put in the charge of any officer of the district whose duties or office facilities best fit him for the purpose, whether it be the warden of a ward, the clerk or treasurer of a city, or whatever officer of a town or precinct the law may either designate or authorize each municipality to select for itself. Such officer shall be required, for a certain number of consecutive days or evenings, to provide two ballot boxes, marked respectively with the names of the two leading parties at the last election preceding, for the reception, under the usual regulations against fraudulent voting, of names of candidates to be voted for at the next subsequent election. As each legal voter deposits his ballot, the presiding officer shall check his name in the list with the letter indicating into which box it was cast, as " R " for Republican, and " D " for Democratic. At the close of the voting period, said officer shall count the ballots in each box, and the highest number in each bearing the same name shall be considered as designating the regular candidate, or, if the ticket embraces more than one name, candidates of each party; and the officer shall so make and publish the sworn returns in any manner which may be directed by law.

To provide for the exigency of third or new parties, said officer shall be empowered to open other additional ballot boxes, whenever a legally designated proportion of the whole number of voters in the district—say one-twelfth—shall so petition him in writing, and he shall label said box or boxes as the petitioners may request. A like petition shall cause him to substitute any party name for that which was used at the preceding election.

ITS ADVANTAGES.

Among the obvious advantages of this proposed system are the following:—

First. It sweeps away the whole nuisance and vice of packing. There is no assemblage to pack with adherents collected and distributed by stealth and wielded like an implement; there is no chairman to be secured in advance, with his often controlling influence over the result; there are no committees to be previously " cut and dried." Every citizen would go to the ballot-box separately, and if he did not throw in an honestly chosen ballot, it would be his own fault. He could not be out-manœuvred, brow-beaten, or deceived—that is, through any fault of the system. As an individual, he might beforehand be exposed to misleading and corrupting influences, but these are inherently incident to free society, while it is believed that the plan proposed will be found, on the strictest examination, to have reduced them in the greatest practicable degree. At any rate, one of the worst of the whole class of abuses which the caucus system has directly superadded to our political life is hereby extinguished.

Secondly. The plan avoids all those pernicious or misguiding influences which are peculiar to public gatherings where immediate action is to be taken by the masses. It requires nothing to be done " under the excitement of the moment." There is no speech-making, and no exposure to sudden bias of any kind; there are no facilities for " log-rolling" and no temptation to fall in with the momentary current, whether accidental or contrived. It is true, the ballot-boxes may be surrounded by those who will seek to influence the honest voter. He can hear whatever is said to him and can hold consultation with his friends, or, on the other hand, he can simply hold his tongue, deposit his ballot, and withdraw. It is evident that a plurality gained through this method would be more creditable to the nominee and more truly expressive of the sentiment of his party than the usual majority of the caucus system, for it would be just that plurality which, under the latter system, *ought* to ripen into a majority, but would by no means be sure of doing so.

Thirdly. The plan proposed would cut off opportunities for the perpetration of the grosser kinds of electoral frauds, such as ballot-stuffing and the falsification of returns. We have not dwelt upon these thus far, because there is nothing peculiar in their adaptation to primary meetings, and because the actual resort to the multiplicity of more refined artifices referred to above would seem to indicate that these ruder sorts had come to be regarded as not generally available. Nevertheless, it is obvious that for all this class of frauds, an ordinary caucus presents far greater facilities than a well-conducted election, than which no better preventive has yet been found, and all the safeguards of which, it is believed, are embodied in our plan.

Fourthly. There are obvious advantages in the prolongation of the time for voting. It dissipates many of the extraneous influences injurious to the elector, that would otherwise be brought to bear upon him. Were the balloting to be confined to a single day or evening, the attendant excitement would be powerfully concentrated, and the simultaneous gatherings of both parties would be in danger of renewing, in another form, some of the most objectionable appliances and workings of the caucus system. But with the time extended over two, three, or four days, there would not be gathering enough at any one time to make any such results possible. Again, it would be a convenience to the voter, who cannot always attend a caucus meeting at the hour appointed, or stay during the whole evening, as is often necessary. But with the opportunity thus prolonged, he could nearly always find it convenient to go to the voting-place, especially as one minute would suffice to perform his duty there.

Finally. The plan is simple, inexpensive, and accordant with the habits of our people and the genius of our institutions. It is simple, because the average voter can understand it at once and comply with it, and the average officer can readily discharge all the duties involved in its execution. It is inexpensive, for it requires—though in some cases it may be deemed advisable to create special offices— no new officials, and makes but a trifling addition to the labors of those already employed. It agrees with the habits and institutions of our communities, as it simply seeks to realize, through the familiar methods of the ballot, the democratic principle that every elector is interested in, and ought to enjoy the best facilities for the selection of candidates for office. The legal part of its machinery is only so much as is necessary to impart regularity and authenticity to its action, without trenching upon the voluntary principle in the least. It leaves undisturbed all those agencies of the press, of public meeting and private effort so indispensable for maturing public opinion, and merely confines itself to securing, so far as is possible, the unbiassed expression and the effectual application of that opinion.

POSSIBLE EXTENSIONS OF THE PLAN.

In our development thus far of the plan proposed, we have had in view mainly the nomination of candidates at first hand, so to speak, that is, of candidates who are selected directly by the people, and not by delegates chosen for that purpose. But the selection of these delegates comes naturally within the scope of the plan, which might extend no further, on the ground that, where the delegates to a higher convention are rightly and fairly chosen, there is not much danger of their going astray, as they would only thence be exposed to the usual temptations of assemblies, mitigated in that case by the superior character of the members. But it might be thought advisable, either for the sake of guarding against even these temptations, or of bringing the whole range of nominations closer to the people, or of saving time and trouble, to make the plan include the selection of candidates for county and State offices, for Congress, and even for the Presidency and Vice-Presidency of the United States. The ballots for the nomination of either or any of these officials could, in case the public had been duly notified, be deposited at the same time, even making a part of the same ticket, with those for local nominations; or, special nominating elections might be ordered, as the laws of each State should authorize. It would only be an extension of the same principle, leading to no confusion or difficulty in its regulation. In many parts of the country it is already as urgently demanded as any local or primary reform, and, perhaps, it would be productive of as much satisfaction and benefit to the people. But we need not dwell upon this point. The plan itself is the main thing; and how far it promises to prove efficient, and at the same time to avoid the manifest defects, abuses, and evils, which have brought the caucus system into general disrepute, is left to the candid consideration of the American public, who will never let this subject rest till some adequate reform is wrought out.

ON THE

LEGAL ORGANIZATION OF THE PEOPLE

TO

SELECT CANDIDATES FOR OFFICE.

BY

C. GOEPP,

OF THE NEW YORK BAR.

"INCORPORATE THE PEOPLE."

ON THE

LEGAL ORGANIZATION OF THE PEOPLE TO SELECT CANDIDATES FOR OFFICE.

WHAT is inherent in the nature of man cannot be confined to the United States of America. The other countries of the earth are afflicted with grave political evils; but the peculiar corruption under which we labor is found here only. It is not, therefore, essentially human; and the question correctly stated, must be, is it essentially American? Is it the necessary offspring of human nature, subjected to the conditions imposed by the American form of government? Or is it the result of some unessential feature of our system, some excrescence which might be lopped off, or some hiatus which may be filled without detriment?

That cannot be essentially American which is not found everywhere in America, and which was not known anywhere in America at certain times. But it is freely admitted that the political corruption of the present day is less than forty years old, that it is but little known in New England, and not at all in the part of the country heretofore known as the South; that in the main it has been confined to the belt of country lying between Canada and the Potomac, and the projection of that zone westward. These facts narrow the original query still further in important particulars. It can only read thus: "Is the prevailing political corruption the necessary offspring of human nature subjected to conditions imposed by the American form of government as affected by the geographical or other peculiarities of the belt of country just indicated, and by historical influences which, having come into effect some forty years since, must henceforth operate for ever and ever?"

We are thus led to inquire, theoretically, what is the essence of our polity, and what are its mere accidents?

Representative self-government is the term by which we are accustomed to designate the vital peculiarity of the institutions of this country. Here, as elsewhere in Christendom, the will of the individual is controlled by the power of the State. In the States of continental Europe the tendency is to extend and intensify this supervision, and to frown upon whatever interferes with it. "The greatest enemy," said Napoleon, "of the national spirit, of the general idea of liberty, is the private interest of families and localities"—an index of his notion of liberty.

Among us the control of the State is sedulously excluded from every sphere of human action in which its public usefulness has not been generally recognized, leaving the sphere of individual self-government as large as possible. Where it is found unavoidable to circumscribe the self-control of the individual, he is consulted, equally with his fellows, and required to submit to such decrees only as have the sanction of the majority of the community consisting of himself and of his fellows. But the larger the number of the individuals who vote, the smaller is the relative weight of the individual voter. This is felt as an evil to be confined within the straitest practicable limits: Hence the tendency to leave as much as possible of what must be consigned to governmental care to the administration of the smallest possible political aggregation of individuals—a *township*, a *village*, or a *borough*. Only those functions which remain after satisfying this inclination are handed over to the government at large; and here, direct participation by the individual citizen in the acts of government being impracticable, its place is supplied by a representation.

Partly to facilitate this representation, and partly to carry out still further the policy of reposing the greatest possible share of governmental action in the smallest possible aggregations of population and territory, a system of *counties* and *States* is interposed between the townships and the general government. In so far as the principle is not departed from in the application, nothing capable of being regulated by the county is referred to State regulation, and nothing admitting of regulation by the State is assigned to the functions of the central administration. Thus, while the individual, the township, the county, the State, and the Union present an ascending scale in point of authority and controlling power, the scale descends in respect of the quantity of functions which the policy of the law confers.

Such is the essence of our form of government, from which the practice deviates widely. In Pennsylvania, for instance, the recognized political agency of the township has shrunk to the smallest proportions; and if its virtual influence is still considerable, the fact is owing solely to the irrepressible genius of the institution. The result of this stunted development of the township has been to multiply the functions of the larger organizations, in which representation is necessary. Thus representation is made even more powerful, for weal or wo, than under the theory of our government it ought to be; and the integrity of that representation becomes a matter of vital consequence. Where the machinery by which representation is effected is rude and inefficient, the government fails to be a self-government by the people through their representatives, and degenerates into a government by the spurious representatives over the people. Hence the question of the necessity of corruption is a question not of the principle of representative self-government, but of the machinery by which that principle is reduced to practice.

The vice of our present machinery for effecting the representation of the people is most happily pointed out by the resolution in response to which these lines are penned. Instead of *selecting* representatives we undertake to *elect* them. A mere election, that is to say, a mere count of votes, particularly where it can be but once exercised in effecting a choice, is as awkward a means of choosing as a lottery. To result in a *selection*, that is to say, in an intelligent designation, a canvass must be preceded by deliberation, and by nominations; and there must be an opportunity of voting repeatedly, to combine minorities into a majority. These indispensable requisites, ignored by the law, are at present accomplished by voluntary organizations. But these lawless surrogates for a proper legal machinery have slipped into the grasp of outlaws, under whose manipulations the representatives, intended to be the organs of the self-government of the people, have become their adversaries. And the remedy desired is one which shall restore and perpetuate the harmony of interests between the people and the functionaries delegated to act in their behalf. The origin of the evil is found, therefore, in the absence of a legal organization of the people for the purpose of making themselves truly represented. If the introduction of such an organization is impossible, then the evil must remain.

The problem is a legislative one. We are called upon to modify the organic law. To do that wisely we must leave unaltered the existing law in every particular which admits of being retained, but expunge from the statute book everything incompatible with the end in view; hence the existing law must be studied historically in its origin, its growth, and its effects. Let us inquire how our form of government came into being, and how the abuses now complained of have crept in; in order, if possible, to ascertain whether they are inseparable from the necessary growth of the system as developed through the whole geographical extent and throughout the history of the country, or whether they have ensued upon accidental, temporary, or local departures from the fundamental principle. In so doing we shall test the correctness of our opinion of the practicability of a reform as deduced from the mere theory of our system.

Familiar as we are with this idea of representative self-government, far from being a simple one, it is highly composite, and its realization is the work of history from early times. It is instructive to ascertain the absence of its germs in the states of antiquity; to trace the gradual evolution and combination of its elements from state to state and from age to age, until we arrive at its general recognition in the early decades of the present century; and to note its partial obscuration in the latter stages of the politics of this country.

The rudiment of all republican government is the general sense of a common interest in the conduct of affairs of state. This public spirit is the only practical legacy left us by what we habitually regard as the cradles of civil freedom, the towns of ancient Greece. In every one of them the market-place was the focus of life and intercourse, and in the market-place politics constituted the leading topic of discussion. But on this common ground democracy, oligarchy, and tyranny had equal footing. No rights were recognized, either of persons, of classes, or of municipalities: power laid its heavy hand where it listed, with violence or fraud alone to combat it. Slavery, the oppression of foreigners and denizens, and the subjection of woman, were recognized as lying at the base of their polity. Citizenship depended upon birth, freedom, wealth, and schooling. City warred upon city, as savage wars against savage. The decay of Greece is not proof that citizens ought to remain indifferent to the affairs of their country—that "a young man had better not meddle with politics," but it should teach us that mere political agitation is of no value without a sense of justice to direct, and good faith to control it.

The Roman polity improved upon the Grecian in recognizing a system of private and public rights, derived from a higher source than the mere caprice of the legislator. The liberty of the Roman citizen was not a privilege conferred upon individuals by the accident of public favor, nor, when acquired, were its attributes liable to curtailment by the same precarious influence. It belonged to all who came within the purview of the law, and the law protected what it bestowed. Even the condition of the enemies overthrown in war, though dictated by the conquerors, fortified with legal safeguards, was no less certain and fixed, and often, for that very reason, more desirable than the independence to which it succeeded.

This pervading recognition of principle gave to the Roman republic that universality which enabled it, alone among the constitutions of antiquity, to burst the trammels of locality, to go beyond the city's walls, and to invest with the dignity of citizenship, tribes and nations who had never seen her market-place. "The public are requested to show senators the way to the Capitol" was the sneer of the aristocrats when Cæsar made senators of his "Barbarians." This ridiculed liberality was the real source of her empire. The legions could never have been recruited from the population of the original town; every conquered people supplied the materials for further conquests. But the military service of these conquered tribes was only secured, or, at least, only made useful, by the loyalty purchased by conferring well-defined rights, and guarding them against violation. "Parcere subjectis, ac debellare superbos."

We are accustomed to regard "liberty protected by law" as a fundamental requisite of happiness; so far as this is true, we owe the lesson to the example of ancient Rome; but what we owe to Rome is more than respect for liberty protected by law. *Law*, meaning the mandate of the legislator, which may be wrong, and yet claim obedience, is not an equivalent for the *jus* of the Latin tongue. Roman liberty rested upon recognized rights, older than legislation, and which legislation may protect and develop, but cannot originate. "*Liberty on principle*" is the great Roman doctrine, which the modern world has done well to receive, and in the study of which it will do well to persevere.

The defect of the Roman system was its want of representation. Aristotle teaches that a State (by which, of course, he means a city) must be neither too large nor too small. It should not be so large but that all the citizens may be acquainted with each other, "*for how else can they select their magistrates?*" An argument doubly cogent, when we consider that Aristotle's citizens, like Calhoun's, excluded the working classes. The citizens of Rome were counted by millions, and were separated by distances requiring journeys of months to overcome; yet they could only vote in a single forum, and could not jointly deliberate at all.

The idea of exercising the right of suffrage at more than one spot, or of delegating it to a limited number of men themselves elected, did not occur even to the Italian allies of the republic, when they struck for equal rights, and proclaimed their independence. Never having succumbed to the Roman arms, these cities had done nothing to forfeit the exercise of sovereignty. As allies they were theoretically equals of the Romans, and therefore entitled to a voice in their deliberations respecting war and peace. Yet those deliberations were had only in the Roman market-place, and by Roman citizens. The practical superiority thus reserved, bred the usual insolence and turbulence, culminated in downright oppression, and provoked revolt. Like the rebellious Southerners of our day, the Italians adopted for their government a constitution, modelled in every essential particular upon that of the State from which they seceded. Elevating the little country town of Corfinium to the dignity of *their* Rome, they named it " Italia," and presented themselves with its " Italian" citizenship, in lieu of that Roman citizenship, which the Romans had withheld from them. The forum of Corfinium was to them what the market-place of Rome was to the State on the Tiber. The capital of Italia held the Italian Senate, at whose doors sat the tribunes of the Italian plebs. Though nominally defeated in the social war, the allies were practically successful. The Romans only succeeded in breaking up their confederacy by conferring upon the inhabitants of most of their towns that very suffrage which had been the original subject of dispute. And when, " after the social war," says Blackstone, " all the burghers of Italy were admitted free citizens of Rome, and each had a vote in the public assemblies, it became impossible to distinguish the spurious from the real voter, and from that time all elections and popular deliberations grew tumultuous and disorderly; which paved the way for Marius and Sylla, Pompey and Cæsar, to trample on the liberties of their country, and at last to dissolve the commonwealth."

In point of fact, however, the popular assemblies had been riots from the earliest time. The populace were regaled with stump speeches, but had no means of deliberating among themselves. Forced to act as an unwieldy mass, they could only threaten secession or execute the threat. The tribunate, intended to obviate these turmoils, was itself but a legally recognized sedition, and the veto substantially a cry of revolt. In the effort to convert the tribune into an intelligent and efficient organ of the popular will, he was insensibly metamorphosed into an emperor. So inevitable is this result, in a free and ambitious community, spread over a large territory, and deprived of local organs, that the French republic, even though endowed with a fictitious representation, entered upon this transformation almost as soon as it entered upon existence.

The necessity of local organization is the negative lesson derived from Roman experience.

Local organization was the distinctive feature of the conquerors of Rome. The Germans required no city walls and no market-places to secure to every man the right, not only of voting, but of deliberating on public affairs. Their folkmote was not a city rabble, but a staid gathering of friends and neighbors, which not only satisfied the postulate of Aristotle, but went further, in never becoming even so numerous as to induce confusion. The Saxon word "hundred" should have a place in every constitution. It keeps alive the reflection that the efficiency of an assembly depends materially upon the numbers of which it is composed. Madison has well said, " Had every Athenian citizen been a Socrates, every Athenian assembly would still have been a mob ;" on the other hand, less than twenty men, though inspired with the highest aims and entertaining the largest views, will inevitably constitute a clique and not a senate.

Without a distribution into organized hundreds, therefore, the individual citizen is a lay figure, though he cast a thousand votes. A poll has no significance except such as it derives from the deliberations out of which it issues. An election without deliberation is a dumb show, and those who ballot without consultation have been most aptly termed "voting cattle." And even consultation is of comparatively little value, if had between men who are total strangers to each other. The more intimate our acquaintance with those whom we consult, the more just our estimate of what they say, and the greater our facilities for influencing their judgment. The power of aristocracies and oligarchies lies in the concert which grows out of their knowledge of each other; and where democracies degenerate into ochlocracies, it is because the voters pronounced equal in legal theory, never meet as neighbors or acquaintances, or under any circumstances calculated to foster mutual esteem. Where rich and poor come into contact only in the act of dropping bits of paper into the same box, it is inevitable that the two classes should take sides against each other. Where, on the contrary, a hundred men of all conditions habitually meet in the same room, to confer on the same subject, however equal they may be in the number of votes they cast, each soon exercises influence in exact proportion to the impression entertained of his ability and good intentions The result is a compromise between equality of rights and variety of capacities, which endures, because equally consonant to the principles and interests of all parties.

Nor is this the most important reason why a democracy bereft of the institution of hundreds must remain a fiction. Without them you cannot bring the opportunity of political action to every man's threshold. You must leave the political centres, the hearthstones of the republic, so far apart, that the poor man, not favored in point of location, must choose between neglecting his politics and neglecting his daily labor. Wherever churches are so far asunder that the day laborer cannot attend them of an evening without interfering with his work, the fact is recorded in proof of great religious apathy in the community in question. By the same token it argues political apathy to find a people without the means of taking political action, except at the sacrifice of their legitimate business. In a real democracy there should be within a mile of every man's door a stated folkmote at early candlelight, at least once a week, with as many adjourned meetings as the business might require.

The citizens of the latter Roman empire, feeling their political helplessness, had lapsed into political indifference, and thence, inevitably, into cowardice. The foresters of Germany, conscious of their individual sovereignty, fought like men, each of whom expected to conquer an empire for himself. After establishing their supremacy their problem was the reverse of that which the Romans had failed to solve. It was for them to unite their many local organizations into a connected whole, protecting without enthralling, the single parts. At first the camp of the conquering army was the natural point of concentration; and the head-quarters of the general, taking the title of the "court" of the "King," continued to do that office during those intervals of peace, which, in those times, were the exception rather than the rule. There was no law to limit the sphere of action of this institution; and but for the local self-government of the hundreds, it might have ended in oriental despotism. The capitularies of Charlemagne, resting upon no higher sanction than the will of the monarch, assume to regulate all the relations of man and man. But in their provisions the wishes of the people were considered no less than if they had been formally consulted. There was no power to execute them outside of the folkmote. The counts who governed the shires into which the empire was divided, had no force except the militia of the counties themselves, with which to administer domestic government, besides repelling external invasion.

To facilitate the execution of his edicts, Charlemagne devised an expedient, which, possibly without any such design, constitutes the most important epoch in the history of the institutions under which laws are made. At stated intervals he sent "messengers" from his court into the counties, to confer with the counts and the people, enforce the render of services, collect such taxes as were then imposed, most of them payable in kind, promulgate the laws, hold courts, hear grievances, and either redress or report them to head-quarters. This measure altered the county from a mere geographical division into a self-acting municipal institution. The messengers were received by the most influential inhabitants of the county, coming from every part of it, who thus constituted a natural representation of the people. The question of taxation kept alive the consciousness of a common interest as against the government. The coming of the envoys was the occasion for discussing, in this plenary assembly, all the affairs of the shire, for disposing of appeals from the hundred courts, and for addressing the king on subjects of universal interest. A connecting link between the hundreds and the king's court was established on the one hand, and on the other, the vast unwieldy ship of state was divided like a modern steamer into innumerable water-tight compartments, each of which could outlive the scuttling of any of the others, and assist in floating them. The empire of Charlemagne, as an empire, was short-lived, because his successors lacked the ability required to perpetuate the throne. But the institutions on which that throne was reared, and which are really his handiwork, survived for centuries, and furnished the vital germ of those under which we are now living; without them representative government would have been impossible, for there must needs be constituencies to be represented before there can be representation; and the hundreds alone cannot furnish the basis of that representation in a country of any magnitude, without producing a representative body so large as to become in its turn an unmanageable rabble.

In the greater portion of the empire itself, Switzerland and the Netherlands excepted, the counties underwent so many transformations as in course of time to lose entirely their original character; but not before the system had been introduced, by adoption, into two neighboring kingdoms, by the founders of which the great Frankish chieftain was regarded as the highest authority on all matters of government. In England and in Hungary, a thousand years ago, the shires were organized on the plan of Charlemagne, and all local government was vested in the county courts. There the earl and the bishop sat side by side while the body of the county gathered around them, and transacted not only judicial, but, what received far more attention, administrative and legislative business. These two realms are wide apart, and there never was any concert of action between them. Both have at this date the form of government then established. Both have at times lost, apparently, all their self-government in counties. In both, the natural tenacity of the institution has overcome all the ravages of conquest, all the terrors of despotism, and all the arts of administration. A more conservative measure was never devised. It preserves republicanism in the midst of empire, and protects the minority against all the vagaries of party spirit. Among a people enjoying communal self-government in every hundred, arbitrary power will never become intolerable. In a country of self-governing counties, there can be no tyranny of majorities. Where both the hundred and the shire preserve their full authority, there is a self-acting protection against encroachments of every description.

Like the continental monarchs of the same era, the early Norman kings enriched the list of political organizations, as handed down by their Teutonic predecessors, by chartering boroughs and cities. The antique constitutions were purely urban, those of the Teutonic nations, in their origin, exclusively rural; the combination of the two is one of the greatest advantages of modern times over both. It has been effected, however, in an empirical manner, and without any attempt to reduce it to scientific exactness. An urban community requires details of administration radically different from those which answer for a rural one; but this diversity is one of detail merely, not of principle; the functions of both, like the individual rights to be protected by each, essentially correspond, and must be regarded as equivalent. On principles of convenience, therefore, and economy, urban and rural administrations should be distinct from each other; on principles of justice and of public policy their relations should be so adjusted that the inhabitants of the one enjoy the same participation in public affairs as those of the other. Such were not, however, the motives of the Normans in granting municipal franchises. They wanted money; and it was easier to put towns under contribution than country districts. The burghers were anxious to secure the easiest possible terms of payment, and to exercise what influence they could upon the tax collectors. The charter was a compromise by which the king, generally in consideration of a heavy bonus—then called a "fine"—waived the demand of a further irregular tribute, and received the promise of regular contributions, to be assessed upon the citizens by some of their own number.

If the solicitude of the individual for the public welfare, the regard for principle in political affairs, the distribution of power among organized neighborhoods, the subordination of neighborhoods under organized shires, and a proper adaptation of these principles to the peculiar case of urban populations, are the fundamental requisites of free institutions, we find these desiderata satisfied without reference to the long-winded "constitutional" debates which have occupied the ruling classes of Great Britain for seven hundred years, and which those classes are schooled to consider the fountain-head of well-regulated liberty. Nothing in history was ever so different from what it was supposed to be as the British form of government.

In fact, the history of parliament begins at the precise point where the interest of the masses in the subject terminates.

Wherever their exchequer and their authority were not in question, the conquerors kept their promise of "upholding the good laws of King Edward the Confessor." Thus they never interfered with the institution of the hundred, which remained in vigor until the pauperization of the country by Henry VIII., and which, though extinct since the seventeenth century as a political organization, is still recognized as the basis of territorial division for the purpose of deciding questions of settlement under the poor laws. Its decadence keeps even pace with the rise of the plutocracy, which could see nothing to foster in so democratic a regulation.

This plutocracy is the natural result of the governmental rapacity of the Normans. They deserve credit for having established, on impregnable foundations, the equality of all men, not, indeed, before the law, but before the rate collector. In the interest of his exchequer, William the Bastard stripped the shires of their functions of self-government, and made them mere collection districts, sending into each of them, from year to year, a sheriff, as absolute satrap, with no responsibility except a most rigid one to the king's purse, and with no limits to his power as legislator, judge, or executioner. The excess of the evil worked its own cure. The landholders of each county, driven to band together in a common cause, united in remonstrances to the sheriff, and petitions to the king. Themselves the sole military force within reach, they constrained the sheriff to consult when he was most anxious to coerce them. They assisted in assessing the imposts among themselves; they testified and interceded for and against each other, before his judgment-seat. In short, under color of supporting, they measurably controlled the officer of the crown. Their services were gratuitously rendered; the protection of their interests as taxpayers being a sufficient inducement. In consequence, England enjoys to this day, the gratuitous administrative services of her richest men; an advantage only balanced by the circumstance that the administration has always been in the interest of the very rich, and rests upon the pauperism of the country.

The era of reform, if such it may be called, dates from the Constitutions of Clarendon, by which, in the year 1164, Henry II. adjusted his long drawn controversy with the ecclesiastics. That done, he promulgated "the great assize," which all authorities agree in pronouncing the most important law ever made in England, but the text of which has always been reported as lost. Had it been preserved, the judges would have been constrained to expound the branches of the law to which it related, by interpreting its terms; in the absence of the text, their decisions became in themselves the ultimate explorable source of law. It would be indecorous to suspect the judges, advocates, and revenue officers of having intentionally suppressed the statute for any such purpose. But it is certain that while Sir Matthew Hale pronounces the origin of the common law as undiscoverable as the sources of the Nile, we find it administered precisely from the period of the adoption of this vanished enactment.

Whether embraced in the wording of the act or not, the leading maxim of jurisprudence thenceforward observed was, that there should cease to be one code of laws or usages binding upon Normans as such, and another binding upon Saxons as such. Saving the binding force of the *jus gentium* as administered in the courts of admiralty, in matters subject to their jurisdiction, and the binding force of the canon law as administered in the ecclesiastical courts under the provisions of the Constitutions of Clarendon, and the binding force of many local customs, all the realm was now governed by a *law common* to all the king's lieges expounded and (for want of the text of the *magna assisa*) made by the king's court, which acted concurrently with, and in supervision of the sheriffs and their county courts. Recurring, like the contemporary kings of France, to the great institution of Charlemagne, the king's court is represented at each shire town by itinerant justices, who go the rounds of each circuit four times a year, at stated terms. Here they are met by the body of the county, that is to say, by the whole number of those who, holding lands under the king, are bound, at his summons, to attend upon his person. The county tenders indictments of crimes committed, and makes presentment of grievances. The judges question the inhabitants of the respective neighborhoods in regard to disputed facts, and, upon their findings, render judgment, which the sheriff, who has summoned the county, is required to execute. Civil and criminal actions are conducted on the same principles; exchequer cases were long deemed of more importance than either. As the details of the system have come to be perfected, partly by mere usage, and partly by subsequent statutes, the same body of the county, though acting in some matters without the participation of the king's judges, administers the conservation of the peace, the inspection of the militia, the repair and construction of roads and bridges, the relief of the poor, and the repartition of taxes.

These functions, it will be seen, embrace the entire sphere of internal administration. The grand jury, a delegation from the body of the county, took the place of their constituents, and, in presenting grievances, originated legislative as well as administrative measures, the king's court having been reduced at an early period to the functions of a sort of central receiver's office, the exchequer. Under the general supervision of the king's judges and the nominal presidency of the sheriffs, the internal administration is conducted, primarily, by the holders of the king's commission of the peace, who administer the government partly by virtue of their judicial dignity, and partly by force of their social position. What they do is done mainly under the form of adjudications, while, in reality, their decrees are administrative; and as they make precedents of their own acts, they virtually legislate, at least as effectively as the courts of record. On quitting the bench, they go to expound and execute their own regulations, as sole local magistrates, at their respective homes. Here they exercise, in minor matters, the unlimited power of Turkish cadis, hedged in by the divinity of wealth, and the patriarchal splendors of the manor house. A secondary position in this hierarchy of local administration is occupied by the class of the lesser tax-payers, who fill the clerkships and salaried offices, and serve as jurors. The working masses of the people have nothing to do with the body of the county, except to be governed and judged by them, to support them by their labor, and to subsist on their charity.

I have described a system which is radically bad, because plutocratic, which is very good in so far as it carries out, for the classes who control it, the principle of local self-government; which is the form of the British government at the present day; which has grown out of the institutions of Henry II. (copied from those of Charlemagne), without any change except the improvement of details; and which is entirely independent of what is currently worshipped as the corner-stone of English liberties—the Parliament.

That body is an ornamental excrescence on the British constitution, which tends to enhance the dignity of the ruling classes, but in which the people have no interest. If this assertion requires any qualification, it is at least impregnable to this extent, that Parliament wields no power except that which inheres in the local self-governments it represents, and that the chances of the people depend on their acquiring, not a representation in the House of Commons, but a participation in the labors of the Quarter Sessions. Parliamentary institutions have been religiously copied in France, in Prussia, in Spain, and in any number of other countries; nowhere have they withstood either a revolution or a *coup d'état*. The reverse is the case in Hungary, because there, as in England, the Parliament rests, not upon itself or a supposititious public opinion, but upon organized self-governing local communities. England is herself the best proof of this. Charles I. had no difficulty in dispensing with Parliament; his difficulty was that the collection of the taxes and the internal administration could not be wrested from the county sessions. As long as the counties sustained the Parliament against him, it triumphed. The Long Parliament could not have been swept away by a gesture of Cromwell, if it had not undertaken to shake them off, and if they had not proclaimed that "the gods were departing" from it. The Lord Protector lacked the protection of the country party, and they easily restored, not the Stuarts, but themselves.

The kings of England had their council, like other kings; and, like them, they sought to enhance the solemnity of their more important acts, by reciting, and, if possible, securing, the assent of their most influential subjects. The influence of these barons in the county courts was an important consideration in summoning them to advise the king. Like the property on which this influence depended, their place in the council became hereditary. The usurping house of Lancaster was forced to lean on the peers of the realm, and for a time made them a power in the state, but since the accession of the Tudors their importance has depended, not upon their membership of the House of Lords, but on the influence they command in their respective shires. Such is the origin of the Upper House of Parliament.

When, in this country, at the present day, electioneering funds are needed by politicians, the practice is to circulate invitations to the "influential members" of a "great party," to assemble for "important deliberations," and, having thus entrapped the victims, to dine and wine them, if expedient, but at all events to lay them under contribution. It was on this very principle that the early kings of England convoked what has since become the Lower House of the "imperial senate."

The counties assessed and collected the taxes. Therefore, when the exchequer required extraordinary relief, the "*commons*"—by which is meant the counties and the boroughs, to wit, the self-governing *communes* or communities, so organized as to enjoy facilities for raising revenue—were invited by circular to send delegates for the "redress of grievances." The grievance in question invariably proved to be an ebb in the royal strong box. At first the knights and burgesses were not even consulted collectively, but each delegation was regarded as totally disconnected from every other. They found their interest in uniting as a house, and presenting joint petitions, and induced the crown to sanction this pretension by asking the crown to nominate a speaker. It was never necessary for them to *refuse* a subsidy, because, without the *positive* co-operation of their constituents, there would have been no machinery for collecting one, even if the house had voted it. They were in a position to make stipulations, and stipulated successfully, first, for the right to audit the expenditures, then for a consulting voice in the appropriation of the funds, and, finally, for a supervision of the administration. They visited misrule by impeachment, and became the natural organ for demanding changes in the law. The spoils of the monasteries made Henry VIII. and his children nearly independent of the Commons; the Stuarts, finding this treasure squandered, saw their power depart with it. The Hanoverians, feebler than the Stuarts, virtually surrendered even the right of selecting their own advisers. Parliament became "omnipotent" in so far as it had no longer the crown to consider; but its omnipotence was so purely that of the organized constituencies, that it could not quell the revolt of a young colony lying outside of the sphere of those constituencies, and imbued with independent germs of self-government.

Previous to its final recognition, this omnipotence of Parliament was the bone of contention between two parties. When the question was decided, it was found that parliamentary action had engendered parties independently of the existence of a subject of dispute, that the parties remained after the dispute between the Commons and the Crown was ended, and that, for the sake of the parties, new disputes must be provided. To meet this want an issue was made up between that description of tax-payers who pay taxes on real estate, and those who pay taxes on personal property. The latter grew in wealth and relative influence in the large boroughs, and, by consequence, in Parliament. The effort to alter the representation in Parliament so as to conform to the change in the relative wealth of the two classes, was in direct collision with the interests of the "omnipotent" body, as constituted when the innovation was proposed. It was, as a conservative member correctly observed, an invitation to the then House of Commons to commit *felo de se*. If, then, Parliament performed this act of *hari kari*, the indications are strong that its movements are actuated by a power outside of itself. The act has just been repeated; it having been discovered, on the one hand, that a sufficient number of artisans are able to pay taxes to add them to the other plutocratic elements, and, on the other, that a number of poor men are so far dependent on the rich, that they may be trusted to vote in their interest. Further steps in the same direction may be taken hereafter; the distribution of the money power will be readjusted from time to time; but in all probability the plutocratic principle will remain.

For the ruling classes, this form of government is exceedingly desirable, as is best proved by the very harmless character of the imperfections in the system which rise to their consciousness. One of these ought to be the practice of bribing electors; but it is the one of which less is said than of any other. John Adams is reported to have observed, " Purge the British Constitution of its corruption, and give to its popular branch equality of representation, and it would be the most perfect constitution ever devised by the wit of man;"—and Alexander Hamilton to have answered, " Purge it of its corruption, and give to its popular branch equality of representation, and it would become an *impracticable* government: as it stands at present, with all its supposed defects, it is the most perfect government which ever existed." The latter opinion is certainly the more consistent of the two. An avowed plutocracy must be no less anxious to preserve a practical inequality in point of influence between the rich and the poor voter, than between the poor voter and the man too poor to vote at all.

Evils which attract far more attention at the hands of publicists are the disproportion between the number of members representing the various constituencies in Parliament, and the relative populations and wealth of those constituencies; the compulsion imposed upon the voters of each constituency, to choose between the two or three candidates standing for their particular counties or boroughs, and the impossibility of voting with effect, for candidates of a more acceptable shade of opinion, who do not happen to stand for the particular constituency; the necessity imposed on the representative, of consulting the local prejudices, and the wishes of his district as well as his own political doctrines; and the difficulty experienced by scholars, ambitious of political distinction, in inducing local constituencies to vote for them.

" In every parliament," says John Stuart Mill, " there is an enormous fraction of the whole body of electors, who are without direct representation, consisting of the aggregate of the minorities in all the contested elections, together with we know not what minorities in those which, from the hopelessness of success, have not even been contested. All these electors are as completely blotted out from the constituency, for the duration of that parliament, as if they were legally disqualified." And again, "At present, by universal admission, it is becoming more and more difficult for any one, who has only talents and character, to gain admission into the House of

Commons. The only persons who can get elected are those who possess local influence, or make their way by lavish expenditure, and who, on the invitation of three or four tradesmen, or attorneys, are sent down by one of the two great parties from their London clubs, as men whose votes the party can depend on under all circumstances."

But while these reflections occupy the minds of thinkers, the objection to the present political condition of England, uppermost in the minds of the great herd of English politicians, is the tendency towards equality of rights before the public law. Even Mill, in advocating his proposed alteration, argues that "under any suffrage approaching to universal, it would operate in favor of the propertied and of the most educated classes." Mr. Lytton, her Majesty's Secretary of Legation at Copenhagen, wrote to Sir A. Paget, in 1863, " that the danger which must arise of government by a single (and that, on the whole, the least educated) class, has long been apparent;" and " has suggested the necessity of devising, if possible, some modification of the electoral system, calculated to secure a more adequate representation to the interests of minorities." Even the authority of John C. Calhoun has been adduced in support of this consideration.

In this emergency the eyes of the British minority were turned upon Denmark, where the arts by which minorities overrule majorities were studied and practised, for many years, with exceeding assiduity. According to the census of 1860, the entire population of the then monarchy amounted to 2,604,024. It was composed of the Islands and of the Cimbric Peninsula, which latter is divided into Jutland, Schleswig, and Holstein. The Islands were inhabited by Danes, Jutland by Danes with a considerable German admixture, Schleswig by Germans somewhat infused with Danes, and Holstein by Germans. Holstein (including Lauenburg) numbered about 550,000 people; Schleswig, 400,000. The Danes, once the ruling nation of the North, were left, by the peace of 1814, high and dry on the sands of bankruptcy and territorial insignificance. They had lost Norway, and the day was fast approaching when the duchies, recognizing the Salic law of succession, must be severed from the kingdom, in which the female line were capable of inheriting. As yet the Danes enjoyed the advantages of a court, trained in ambitious traditions of a fleet and an army in which they held the commissions, a diplomatic representation and a bureaucracy recruited from their ranks. After pronouncing, in 1844, for the consolidation of the *entire* monarchy, they substituted, in 1848, the project of annexing Schleswig alone, so that they might easily outvote it, leaving Holstein the privilege of being a self-governed dependency, all the more helpless from having a separate legislature, in which the sympathies of the Schleswigers could not aid it. In the war which ensued, they succeeded beyond their hopes, achieving not only the incorporation of Schleswig, but the unity of the succession in the entire monarchy. In October, 1855, they proclaimed the new imperial constitution, and interdicted its discussion by the German provincial assemblies. On the protest of the Germanic Confederation against this act of usurpation, Holstein was again, in 1858, exempted from submission to the new constitution, and thereby severed from her natural ally, Schleswig.

The powers of legislation of the "empire" were vested in a "rigsraad" to be composed of 80 members. Of these 20 were to be appointed by the crown, that is to say, by the Danes; 30 were to be elected by the provincial assemblies; and 30 by the people. Of those elected by assemblies 18 were assigned to Jutland and the Isles, and 12 to the Duchies; those elected by the people were assigned to the two divisions of country in the proportion of 17 and 13. This scheme would have insured at all times 55 Danish to 25 German votes.

But the plan went further. For the purpose of electing the 30 members by direct popular vote the entire monarchy was divided into nine districts, three of which, constituting the Danish region, elected respectively 7, 3, and 7 members, while Holstein, as a fourth district, was called upon to elect 8, and Schleswig was cut up into five districts, each only large enough for a single member. The non-application of the scheme to Holstein, foreseen from the first, resulted in leaving the German nationality represented solely by the delegates from the five Schleswig districts; or rather from four of them, because even in one of them the majority was Danish.

In these Schleswig districts, the manner of voting was in effect the same as it is in this country. But a different mode was provided for the three districts constituting Denmark proper. Here each voter sent in a written paper, stating, over his signature, his first choice, and as many other preferences as he happened to have. The voting papers of each district were counted, and the aggregate divided by the number of representatives assigned to the district, the quotient being the minimum number of voters necessary to elect a member. The candidate who was found to be the first choice of the necessary number of papers first opened, was declared elected. The canvass being further prosecuted whenever the candidate already proclaimed as selected reappeared as a first choice, his name was struck out, and the second choice upon the same paper recorded instead. If the first reading of the papers failed to produce a full delegation, each with the requisite minimum of votes, the papers already counted were again overhauled, the second choices being now recorded where the first had been taken before. The further details are not essential.

It is unnecessary to say that under this system the Danish party elected the entire delegation of every district, and that their most active party leaders never failed in polling the largest number of votes. Considering the limits of its actual power, there never was a party which accomplished more than the Eider Danes of 1848. A man differing from them in opinion might possibly have secured a majority in a district embracing one-seventeenth part of the population; but he could never hope to obtain the suffrages of one-seventh of the voters of a district of which the whole kingdom only numbered three. On the other hand, if Holstein had submitted, it is quite probable that the officials, government dependents, and Danish residents in that duchy might have mustered in sufficient force to carry one or two of the eight representatives assigned it.

The plan thus introduced by Mr. Andrae, the Danish minister of finance, in 1855, is not materially variant from the one since suggested in England by Mr. Thomas Hare, of London. Both, as has been well remarked by Mr. Simon Stern, of New York, the ablest advocate of their leading ideas in this country, require too much machinery to be practicable in this country. That gentleman offers a material improvement upon either. "The State of New York," he says, "has about 800,000 voters; divide this by 128, the number of seats in the Assembly, and you have a quotient of a trifle over 6000 votes necessary to elect a representative, as the minimum number of proxies or powers of attorney from individual voters, necessary to entitle a candidate to a seat. Every person receiving a larger number of votes than this minimum should be deemed elected, and should cast, in the legislative body, upon every measure coming to a vote, the number of ballots cast for him, and which he represents, be they six thousand or twenty thousand."

This is certainly a direct, simple, and satisfactory mode of doing what both Andrae and Hare effect imperfectly, at an enormous expense of time and trouble. It strikes us as the perfection of mathematical politics.

But all these proposals appear to us to confound the distinction between these two subjects of thought. It is the general tendency of them all to delocalize representation. Any of them, if adopted in England, would probably diminish the seeming importance of Parliament by dissociating it from the localized distribution of power which actually controls the body politic; but would not necessarily interfere with the self-government of the country as vested in the local administration of the counties and boroughs. The case would be altered, if the plan were pressed for acceptance upon a country like the United States, in which local self-government is less perfectly developed, in which power, so far as not secreted in irresponsible party combinations, really reposes in the legislative assemblies, and depends for its local distribution upon the continuance of the merely territorial divisions out of which the representatives are selected.

A year or two before the accession of Count Bismarck, a writer on German politics argued that if a German Parliament were desirable at all, it should not be composed of representatives from local municipalities, which, among a people so long estranged from the practice of self-government, had necessarily lost all political address, but of delegates from the innumerable social orders, ranks, classes, trades, professions, guilds, and innings, into which that unfortunate nation is dismembered. Not only, in his opinion, should the nobles have representatives of their own, and the clergy, but the universities, the doctors, the office holders, the schoolmasters, the merchants, the manufacturers, the tailors, the shoemakers, the day laborers, the barbers, the footmen, the seamstresses, and the servant girls. The suggestion has never been tested in practice; but to an American mind a gathering of persons representing such divers and strongly marked opinions and interests, would seem to derive no advantage from consultation. Each member would come to the consideration of every question with his mind irrevocably made up, and with no choice except between impracticability in his intercourse with his colleagues and infidelity to those who had sent him. Such a state of things would present temptations to corruption from which our present system is exempt.

Would not Mr. Hare's measure effect just what the German writer sets out with proposing? Of the many parties desiderated by the former, as many, if possible, as there are representatives for spokesmen, a large number would be formed, at first, upon the issues under discussion before the change. But conflicting business interests would influence more and more, and finally control, the transformation of parties. That point reached, the legislature would become impervious to argument, because each member would be chained to the particular interest electing him. Yet the contest would go on; if not with arguments, with what weapons would it be waged? Business interests are moneyed interests. Among the constituents and among the members, the effort, having ceased to be to confute, would be to outbid; and in the end *doctrinaires* might be found to declare this species of influence strictly legitimate. "*Vous sentez vous corrompus?*"

Mr. Hare assumes that the politics of a free country must be conducted in the shape of a contest between parties; that every citizen must belong to some party; that the existence of two parties only is a badge of rudeness; that the tendency of political civilization is to increase the number of parties; and that the highest point of development attainable is that in which every member of the legislature represents a party of his own. It may be useful to examine these postulates in the light of history.

The people of England were not always divided into political parties; the Whigs and Tories date from the period when the House of Commons had attained a recognized position as the arena of political strife. While the power of Parliament was derived from the local constituencies, the spirit of party entered the local constituencies by emanation from Parliament. The existence of parties in Parliament is not remarkable. Where majorities rule there will be efforts to obtain majorities; and the effort to obtain a majority, so soon as it is not confined to a single casting of votes, is an effort to form a party. Before the days of the Tudors each county doubtless had its division into parties, and each hundred must have had them in the days of Edward the Confessor; but these parties were formed upon issues more or less local, with little reference in one locality to the divisions formed in another, and often without any reference to the election of the member for Parliament, then treated as a merely incidental matter The members, therefore, had little occasion to introduce the local bickerings into their debates. On the other hand, the parliamentary parties were strictly incidental to the business of Parliament, and it was irrational to carry them to the hustings; nor was that change effected without an entire and a mischievous departure from what these parties had previously been, and from what, in their nature, they ought to be. Nothing is more immediately practical, more dependent on innumerable circumstances and conditions, more subject to fluctuation, than the combinations into which a voter should enter with his fellow voters, and from which he shoud recede, as the course of political events and political deliberations progresses. Every poll is had partly with reference to the effect it will produce upon the combinations of voters at subsequent polls. Hence, there should be, in strictness, a recast of parties after every poll. If, therefore, the constituencies are to participate in the party contests of their representatives, they can do so fairly under no condition other than that of being permitted to hold fresh elections after every vote cast by their representatives. To do that they must be better organized than are the county constituencies of England, or than Mr. Hare proposes to organize them. As these could speak but once between two dissolutions of Parliament, they could speak only on the fiction that parties are formed on permanent abstractions, capable of being embodied in rigid instructions, and incapable of development or essential modification by any events occurring between one election and another. To cover up these palpable incongruities, it was found useful to "keep out of politics," *i. e.*, out of the charmed circle of these unreal contests, all "practical" matters, that is to say, all matters upon which a free people, governing themselves, ought to reason together; and it became important to carry the whole subject of party politics as far out of the domain of calm reflection, and as far into that of passion and imagination as possible. Parties had to receive names; names had to be coupled with abstractions; abstractions made palpable by the use of colors, signs, symbols, nicknames, and caricatures; these made interesting by fomenting bigotry and fanaticism; and these again turned to practical account by identifying them with the names of candidates.

Such is the ideal basis upon which Mr. Hare desires to erect his edifice. If it really constituted the foundation of England's government, it would long since have proved its grave. But, in fact, it lies only on the surface. The local magistrates administer the essentials of government at their country houses, without reference to the wordy war of politics. They keep themselves before the people as leaders of both parties, and, as such, and by the members whom they elect, take care to keep the abstractions which they preach out of the statute book. The perils of the system become apparent where these checks are wanting; where the division of parties is accepted and practised in good faith; where the parties are formed not inside but outside of the parliamentary bodies, and outside of the constituencies; where parties adopt hierarchical organizations, not serving, but commanding the individual voter; where they nominate, not representatives only, but executive and even judicial officers, and prescribe the measures of government; where they formulate creeds and coerce the conscience; where the voter foregoes all opportunity of voting for or against distinctive measures, and has Hobson's choice between parties only; where parties appeal from the ballot to the sword, while at the same instant the hostile party-managers fraternize in the division of the spoils. If such a state of things is to be mended by multiplying parties, parties should be multiplied; but the premises should be scrutinized before adopting the conclusion.

Furthermore, Mr. Hare assumes that party politics consist in the imposition of pledges by the constituency and in the redemption of those pledges by the representative. It is submitted as the lesson of experience, that the pledges exacted are usually absurd, or manifest themselves as such in the course of events very shortly after having been given But whether absurd or not, it is equally the lesson of experience that they are broken as surely as they are made. This is the real seat of the disease; and this Mr. Hare leaves untouched. He admits that, as matters now stand, the minority is permitted to vote; but he contends that the minority voter is nevertheless disfranchised *for the duration of any parliament* in which his vote has not contributed to elect a member. He contends that the minority voter would not be disfranchised if he contributed to send a member, although for the duration of that Parliament, his member should be outvoted on every division. If these distinctions are sound, why not others? Is not the majority voter now disfranchised for the duration of the Parliament, if his representative, after being elected, votes contrary to his wishes? And would not his minority voter be exposed to the same risk, though enjoying the advantages of the proposed reform? For this evil, then, his scheme furnishes no remedy. And is not such a remedy precisely that of which we are in search?

When Mr. Hare argues that a legislator should represent a totality, he is right; but he thereby condemns his own system. A numerical aggregate of individuals is not a totality, but a multiplicity, no matter how similar their opinions. A totality, if consisting of more than one individual, must consist of an organization, and the organization alone is the totality.

> "Sonst hast du die Theile wohl in der Hand,
> Fehlt aber immer das geistige Band."

And if the organization is fairly represented, the totality is represented, although represented by one who differs in opinion from a large number of the individuals composing it. Now, we find society divided into these totalities, in the shape of communes, that is to say, of cities, boroughs, counties, and townships. Their existence is not only actual and real, but necesssary. Towns had governments before counties had. Counties, under the name of tribes, cantons, shires, lands, and clans, were of earlier growth than nations. The smaller organizations are more tenacious of life than the larger. The cities of Italy have preserved their identity, while the Roman republic and empire, the Lombard kingdom, the German empire, the Spanish, French and Austrian supremacies have come and gone. Athens is still Athens, though Greece became Macedon; and Macedon, Rome; and Rome, Constantinople; and Constantinople, Turkey; and Turkey is again becoming Greece. We could not, if we would, extinguish these living totalities by dissociating representations from them. If, therefore, we raise up new factitious totalities for purposes of representation, we juxtapose two sets of totalities, of which the hardier will survive.

Mr. Mill answers this objection by saying, "the interests and feelings of localities always will be represented, because those interests and feelings exist in the minds of the electors. I do not know what better guardian of a feeling can be wanted than the man who feels it. Indeed it may be set down as certain that the majority of voters in every locality will prefer to be represented by one of themselves, or one connected to the place by some special ties. It is those who know themselves to be locally in a minority, and unable to elect a local representative of their opinions, who could avail themselves of the liberty of voting on the new principle. As far as the majority were concerned, the only effect would be that their leaders would have a greatly increased motive to find out and bring forward the best local candidate that could be had."

This motive would be strong indeed. If the party having the majority in the country, had, as is usual, a majority in many localities, and relied upon those local majorities, while their opponents based their organization upon a disregard of localities, the minority might easily elect more members than the majority. Perhaps this is what is intended; but it might be called a slight *over-enfranchisement* of the minority. At all events it exhibits the speciousness of the remark, that the feeling of locality must be safe in the hands of the voter who feels it. The safety of the *feeling* is of no use, if the locality is in jeopardy. The feeling of honesty is safe in the hands of the individual voter; yet he is none the less defrauded by the man to whom he gives his suffrage. It is not a question of *liberty*, but of *facilities*. In the matter of liberty we can never go beyond the principle of universal suffrage; but that principle, without being trenched upon, may be shorn of its efficacy, for want of the proper method of carrying it into practice.

While the parliamentary government of Great Britain has grave faults of its own, it has certainly eschewed most of the ailments which infest our body politic; and this exemption presents itself in conjunction with a system in which the representatives, unlike ours, are selected by distinct, well organized, and powerful constituencies, accustomed to governmental action, and led by men of political experience and marked political opinions. The form of election, it is true, is tumultuary; the individual voter has no recognized means of conferring with his fellows, and is driven to a choice between two evils. The formal nominations and the formal oratory, which precede and accompany the dumb show of voting, do not alter its character, and there are no legal means of enforcing the fidelity of the representative to his constituents, or to the policy which elects him. But the great inequality of social conditions affords the parties a self-sustaining organization, and furnishes them with "natural leaders" amenable to public opinion, and above the lowest grade of temptation. Hence the candidates are not below the common average of respectability, and at least of mediocre parts; some of the best statesmen of the country find constituencies; and arguments addressed to the common welfare have a chance of consideration.

If there is any correctness in the view of English institutions here taken, it must be admitted that our American form of government was modelled not more upon what the British constitution is, than upon what it was supposed to be. This imaginary British government has been so much bewritten and bespeeched, as to be, for many purposes, of almost equal importance with the real one. Several years after the establishment of the Great Assise the barons extorted from King John a promise that he would respect the law as instituted by his predecessor, and would not relapse into the arbitrary despotism of the earlier kings. The subjects thereby ratified the enactment of the great assise, and demanded its perpetuity; a momentous declaration, worthy of being inscribed upon a great charter; but quite unlike the "principles of constitutional government" afterwards interpreted into that famous document. For many years it was not even supposed to bind the crown. Henry III. repealed the charter without objection from any quarter; and afterwards re-enacted it, not as an act of duty, but as of his free will and pleasure. But it was ever the policy of the commons to dignify their encroachments on the prerogative with the mantle of a pretended vindication of prescriptive rights, and the historical lore of the times was not proof against these sophistries. The "Witenagemote," "Edward the Confessor," "trial by peers," and other catch words, served their turn. The Lancasterians claimed to be the champions of these ancient liberties. Sir John Fortescue, the tutor of Henry VI., when in exile, wrote his book "*De Laudibus Legum Angliæ*," and constructed what may be called the platform of the Whig party, of such planks as the maxim that the king cannot alter the law, nor levy taxes without the consent of the Commons, and that he ought not to sit in judgment in person, nor dispense with the agency of a responsible minister. He likewise originated the misunderstanding and consequent abuse of the word "commons," as though instead of meaning communes, or communities (Latin *communa*), it were a categorical opposite to the term "lords." His dogmas, though advanced on his own sole responsibility, were adopted, on account of their utility, as if really consecrated by the combined wisdom of Hengist and Horsa, and all their pikemen. They were in the minds of those who conducted the debates respecting the efficacy of royal proclamations and the validity of irrational acts of Parliament in the time of Lord Coke; and of those who drew and advocated the bill of rights. They swayed the spirits of Noyes, of Hale, of Hyde, and of Somers, and thus outlived as well the Stuarts as the commonwealth. Strafford disputed them, and was beheaded for it. The theories thus contrived for party use in England fell into the hands of Montesquieu, to be improved for other party purposes in France; were retransported to England by De Lolme, and worked up into the first systematic attempt of a literary man to delineate the British Constitution; and underwent further manipulations just before the separation of the American colonies, in Blackstone's primer of English law.

Such was the source from which the school of public men who built up the American republic derived their ideas of what the English form of government was, and of what it should be. Even at home the accuracy of the portrait was devoutly believed in; how could it be suspected by young lawyers in the colonies, who had never seen the original? The fathers of the revolution made that a truth for us which had been but a dream for Englishmen. The colonies, as they entered the revolution, were really little constitutional monarchies, in which there was no taxation without representation, with representative assemblies embodying the political will and action of the people, and governing them in their name, and with reference to their wishes. When they came to erect a general government for themselves, it was precisely such a conglomerate of monarchy, aristocracy and democracy, as Montesquieu, and De Lolme, and Blackstone, supposed the government of Great Britain to be; and this central government in its turn influenced the further development of the state politics. While, however, the conscious acts of the statesmen of the revolutionary period proceed upon this illusory theory of the British Constitution, the natural course of tradition was at work, and, unobserved by politicians, reproduced the substantial features of the actual British form of government. These institutions had immigrated from the first, as matters of course, attracting so little attention that it is difficult, at present, to trace their growth. Thus the institution of the hundred, on the point of extinction in Old England, was transplanted by the pilgrim fathers, and became the corner-stone of the new edifice.

Palfrey informs us that " the institution of towns had its origin in Massachusetts, and was borrowed thence by the other colonies." " In the development of a system, coeval with the settlement of the country, the whole inhabited territory of New England is laid off into these little municipalities. Each town is a body politic, with an administration of its own, conducted by officers of its own choice, according to its will, except as that will is restrained within limits prescribed by the higher common authority. A town is in law a corporation, with rights and liabilities as such, capable of suing and subject to be sued in the courts in disputes with any parties individual or corporate. A town is obliged by law to protect health and quiet within its borders by means of a police; to maintain safe and convenient communication about and through its precincts, by roads and bridges; to furnish food, clothing, and shelter to its poor; and to provide for the instruction of all the children of its inhabitants, at the common charge. Besides occasional meetings, the voters of a town come together once every year to choose the administrators of its business, and determine the amount of money with which it will intrust them, and how this shall be raised. If a general tax is levied, the proportion assessed in each town is paid from the town treasury, the townsmen, by their assessors, distributing the burden of the payment among their own people. On matters of their own interest, the towns present their petitions, and as to matters of general concern, they send their advice to the general authorities. By their magistrates they supervise the elections, alike, of municipal officers, and of all others designated by popular choice."

" This institution," says Bancroft, " was New England's glory and its strength. It was incessantly deplored by royalists of late days, that the law which confirmed these liberties had received the unconscious sanction of William III., and the most extensive interpretation in practice. *He that will understand the political character of New England in the eighteenth century must study the constitution of its towns.*" Nor, let us add, is it only the political character of New England in the eighteenth century that can be thus understood, but also the secret of her preponderance in the nineteenth. Neither in numbers, nor in strength, nor in courage, nor in intelligence, do the Yankees rank so high among the component elements of this people, as to account for the leading position they have achieved; it is the art of combined action acquired in the practice of the town meetings, and the universal understanding of popular interests, only to be obtained where the humblest citizen has an equal hearing, which lie at the foundation of their weight in our national councils.

South of Mason and Dixon's line, we find but scanty traces of any subdivision of the counties; but there, originally, the counties themselves were so thinly inhabited, and the planters, with their large estates, were so intimate with each other, that the counties might have been called hundreds in disguise. They bore, however, the aristocratic type of the English county organization, and absorbed their full share of the functions of local government. The magistrates served gratuitously; and at one time the bench of each county formed a close corporation, and filled vacancies occurring in their own number. Thus were generated the "first families" and all their train; it is hardly fanciful to say that the war just closed has been a war between the county and the town; for although counties have always existed in New England, their political importance there is secondary.

In this struggle between the northeastern and the southeastern type of society, the balance of power was with the Middle States, if we include in that designation the states of the Upper Mississippi Valley. As proprietary colonies the middle provinces of the seaboard had set out in life on a more aristocratic footing than even Virginia, and no divisions smaller than that of counties were introduced into their first establishment; but their people multiplied so rapidly that, from the necessity of the case, townships soon began to be formed. Many of the immigrants spoke a foreign language, and came from countries where every trace of popular self-government had been trodden out. The townships, peopled by such men, never assumed the independence and authority of the New England towns. In New York these subdivisions are at present erected by special acts of the legislature; in Pennsylvania the Quarter Sessions of the respective counties have made and unmade townships from time immemorial, without, so far as known, any other than common law authority for so doing. In both of these communities the division of functions seems to have been made with a view to giving the un-English citizen facilities for participating in the doings of the lesser subdivision, while reserving for the larger all that requires a command of language and skill in affairs.

In Pennsylvania the townships have some jurisdiction over the

schools, the poor, the repair of roads, and the petty police. The
Quarter Sessions have administrative functions very similar to
those exercised by the same bodies in England; but without their
social weight or political importance. The grand jury present
what emergencies require governmental action; for some cases,
such as the erection of new county buildings, their presentment is
an indispensable pre-requisite. The court hear the reports of the
constables respecting the observance of the license laws, the sound-
ness of the bridges, and the supply of finger-boards at the cross-
roads. They lay out and vacate townships and roads, build and
demolish bridges, and license public houses. The county commissioners fix the rates of taxation, superintend the collection, and
make the expenditures. These three bodies together constitute a
county legislature, in point of jurisdiction. The greater accessi-
bility of the State legislature, and the greater equality of social condition between the magistrates on the bench, and the masses of the
people make them more chary of the assumption of responsibilities,
than is the case with the corresponding bodies in England; while
the townships, such as they are, relieve them of some of the details
of administration, which the British county magistrates exercise on
the bench of the Quarter Sessions.

The compromise between the New England and the Virginia
system, thus effected in New York and Pennsylvania, having been
transferred, in its main features, to the valley of the Mississippi,
now prevails in the most populous and wealthy portions of the
Union, and thus the two main pillars of the ancient English commonwealth, the county and the hundred, underlie our own polity as
they do that of the mother country; and we have borrowed from it
the main features of its actual, no less than those of its imaginary
constitution. It is but fair to add, however, that in combining the
advantages of the township and the county as organs of local self-
government, the Middle and Mississippi States have not succeeded
in steering entirely clear of the risk of diluting both of the compo-
nents, without obtaining a combination equally strong with either
one of them, if undiluted. New England and Ancient England have
had a better local system in their towns and hundreds alone, and
Virginia and modern England have better local systems in their
counties alone, than the Middle States have in their townships and
counties as hitherto combined. Neither institution is here quite
as firmly rooted, nor as vigorous of growth, as it should be. Public
attention has not done them justice. During the formation of these
communities, parliamentary bodies, as found in the Federal and State
governments, have been the favorite and recognized organs of public

life. In short, local self-government, while undoubtedly potent here, has been less fruitful of good and has offered less resistance to evil than in New England, in Virginia, or even in Great Britain. Hence it is that the call for the present essay emanates from Philadelphia, and not from Boston or from Richmond. Neither the Eastern States nor what has formerly been called the South, were ever entirely free from political corruption; but it is manifest that the confirmed asphyxia which we are now seeking to remove, is the peculiar product of neither of these two sections, but of the middle and Mississippi States just referred to. Neither the New Englanders nor the Southerners are more virtuous than we of Pennsylvania, New York, Ohio, Illinois, and Missouri; but they are better protected, negatively by their homogeneousness, and positively by the vitality of their local institutions. The impurities of our polity are peculiar, not to human nature, nor to American institutions, but to that portion of our country in which the local self-government of the people has been stunted in its development.

Nor is this by any means the only modification engrafted by us upon the institutions derived from the British Isles. Immeasurably the most important of these alterations is our elimination of the plutocracy of modern England. The members of the municipal councils of our towns and cities appear at all times to have served gratuitously; but they constitute almost the sole exception; even in Virginia the "burgesses," *i. e.*, representatives, always received wages; nowhere (save in our city governments) was power regarded as an adjunct of property, nor attention to the public weal confounded, in theory, with the protection of private interests. This is on the principle that all men are created equal, and that governments derive their just powers from the consent of the governed. The principle of universal suffrage is not guaranteed by the constitution; previously to the rebellion it was unknown in many States, and the great political party of 1787 treated it with derision, and taught that to take care of the rich, and let the rich take care of the poor, was as essential a maxim of our system of government as of that of the mother country. The contrary maxim of Jefferson derives its force only from the fact that it is the sentiment of the people, based on a shrewd appreciation of their own interests, and ratified by the experience of two-thirds of a century. The problem of the propriety of universal suffrage has been thus humorously stated in a private letter written by one of the leading publicists of continental Europe: Does the result show that more are drowned by going into the water before learning to swim, or that more languish on shore because not admitted to the privilege of swimming? The condition of the working classes in America answers the question, and places it beyond the reach of argument or declamation. At this day the principle receives universal homage in clime, which, in the days of its first promulgation, were regarded as the homes of its most formidable enemies. France, Italy, and Germany, have acknowledged, by their own practice, that the plebiscite is the basis of all the ideals of the century. Our own people have just vindicated the principle in opposition to the prejudice of color. It is too late in the day to revert to the prejudice of accumulated wealth. The payment of large taxes argues not a peculiar merit in the taxpayer, but a peculiarly ample share in the fruits of good government. Any taxpayer may relieve himself of his taxes by divesting himself of his wealth; and any non-taxpayer will gladly assume the obligation, if he can acquire the property on which the tax is paid. Man does not belong to property, but property belongs to man. The citadel of corruption with us is found in the municipal council of the large city; precisely at the point where we depart from our principle of compensated political service, and elect aldermen who serve "gratuitously," that is to say, for such bribes as contractors can be made to pay, or, in cases of exceptional honesty, for such speculations as can be made in city real estate by controlling the course of municipal improvement.

The introduction of the ballot in lieu of the registered vote, is coeval with the first settlement of Pennsylvania, Massachusetts, and Virginia. In New York it was regarded as an experiment so late as the Revolution. While it has, by no means, removed all the ills that political flesh is heir to, it cannot fairly be made responsible for any of the particular grievances we are at present laboring to redress; although its introduction serves to mark the increasing disregard of the *deliberations*, however informal, which had theretofore preceded and accompanied the polling of votes, and the gradual disuse of which has given us our present defective method of *election* without *selection*, and decision without deliberation.

Similar in origin was the gradual introduction of election districts, distinct from counties and boroughs. In England, every constituency has one polling place, the hustings, where the nominations are made, the show of hands taken, and the speeches held. In the United States, when such adjuncts came to be discarded, it was natural to consult the convenience of a scattered population, by appointing a number of places for taking votes; and the innovation was only objectionable as tending still further to obliterate the recollection of the original unity and organization of the constituencies.

Another change was the apportionment of representatives according to population. The old English House of Commons was composed of two knights from every shire, and two burgesses from every borough, without any reference to differences in numbers, wealth, or importance. There would have been no equity in taking the population into account, because the suffrage was held by different tenures in every borough. In Pennsylvania, also, the counties were the original constituencies, and originally sent an equal number of representatives. New England had the inestimable boon of organized *towns* for constituencies. But the numerical standard of equity began to encroach upon the principle of independent and integral local organization, when counties in Pennsylvania, and towns in Connecticut, came to be erected, with smaller populations than would have been needed to entitle them, numerically speaking, to at least one representative. In consequence, two counties, or two towns, as the case might be, would be thrown together to form a constituency. From this moment, the organic character was completely lost, and the district became a mere territorial division. As an obvious result of this departure from old landmarks, large counties soon came to be broken up into several constituencies. The adoption of the Federal constitution led, not necessarily but naturally, to a still more settled reception of the purely numerical system, as every Northern State immediately subdivided itself into as many geographical districts as it had congressmen.

Here ensued the abuse of Gerrymandering. Districts, once regarded, not as natural and almost prehistoric individualities, but as arbitrary subdivisions of territory, must be readjusted from time to time, as population alters. This adjustment must be made by law, and therefore under the control of the party prevailing in the legislature. It is in the interest of that party so to arrange the districts as to neutralize the number of the opposing party, massing their votes together in some places where their ascendency cannot be disputed, detaching counties, townships, or wards from their natural connection to destroy an existing majority, or to create it where wanted for party ends; and all this without any regard to territorial contiguity, common interests, or any other consideration but the control of votes. When this practice was in vogue, it was pronounced ineradicable, because grounded upon inextinguishable traits of human nature; but, though human nature survives, gerrymandering has been suppressed, or confined within such limits as to make it comparatively harmless, by introducing the principle that there shall be one separate constituency to each representative, and the principle that each constituency shall be composed of contiguous territory, and shall be compact in form; a return *towards*, if not *to*, the system of integral and organized constituencies. The precedent is of the utmost value; first, as proving that abuses admit of correction, human nature to the contrary notwithstanding, and secondly, in indicating the direction whence relief is to be sought.

Our early institutions varied from those of the mother country in this additional particular, that our elections were not confined to the designation of legislative representatives. Even in England, indeed, some parish officers were always elected. When governors ceased to be sent hither across the ocean, they came to be voted for in the same manner, and at the same time and place as the assemblymen. The Plymouth colony elected a governor in 1624, Massachusetts in 1632, and Connecticut in 1639. Village officers were always elected in the town meetings of New England. In the frame of government first devised by William Penn, and in his constitution of 1690, the freemen of each county are empowered annually to present a double number of persons as candidates for the offices of sheriff, justices of the peace, and coroner, for the year next ensuing; out of which double nominations the governor is to make his selection in three days, and in default of such selection, the candidate first named stands installed. Elective county commissioners of taxes were a recognized institution, at least as early as 1752. The constitution of 1790 retains the provision of its predecessor respecting the election of sheriffs and coroners, but makes all other executive officers, and justices of the peace, to hold by appointment from the governor. The Constitution of the United States raised the superstructure upon this foundation, by making the chief magistrate of the nation, with a patronage which has since proved so enormous, elective by the people.

This is by far the most momentous innovation we have yet noticed, on the institutions borrowed from Great Britain. There the people regard their peculiar liberties as consisting in the right to elect their legislators. In this country they see it in their power to choose their own "rulers." The executive head of the government is so much more conspicuous a personage than any member of a large deliberative body, that his election quite overshadows every other, and that of the representative becomes a matter of secondary consequence. The effect has almost been to substitute an elective monarchy for a representative government; if the chief magistrate held his office for life, it would have had that effect entirely. The effort to prevent such a result, by contracting the power of the governor, so far from raising the relative dignity of the legislature, has tended still further to depress it, by leaving the popular body without a counterpoise to evoke effort, or give an opportunity for the exercise of talent. In the general government, where the president is a powerful monarch, he has always found senators and representatives of talent and of character to cope with; the feeble governors of the States have been pitted against State legislators still feebler, and, too often, of no character at all.

The practice of filling administrative offices by election has led to a further important departure from the old English model, in the system of a tenure of office for stated terms. Members of Parliament were originally elected *pro hac vice*, for the Parliament convoked at the time. The terms of the early Parliaments were so short, that nothing else could have been thought of. When the sessions increased in length and importance, and, especially, when prorogations ensued, the constituencies ought, on principle, to have enjoyed the right of recalling their delegates when dissatisfied with them and of sending others in their places. This was never done, for many reasons, but mainly because the constituencies had not such an organization as to make a revocation practicable. The term of office of a member of Parliament has always lasted as long as the Parliament to which he was elected, and the same rule has obtained in this country. When other offices came to be made elective, the question of the duration of their terms was not controlled by any applicable precedent. It would be jumping to a conclusion to say that a democratic form of government *necessarily* results in filling offices by election for stated terms. The Athenians considered every democracy unsound where the functionaries were chosen otherwise than by lot, because every other method implies that one citizen is better than another. According to our modern ideas, the most democratic arrangement conceivable would undoubtedly be to make the office tenable pending the good-will and pleasure of the authority conferring it, that is, until the whole body of the voters should choose to displace the officer. Where that policy is not adopted, three alternatives remain: the office may be held for life, during good behavior, or for a fixed period. The first tends to make the officer irresponsible; the second, responsible only to the judiciary. In an evil hour the third plan was fixed upon. In all New England elections were annual from the first. This makes the officers, in practice, equally irresponsible with one who holds for life; but the evil is supposed to be abridged because the irresponsible man retires after a stated period. As the effect of the next election, however, is merely to substitute one irresponsible incumbent for another, the irresponsibility is permanent, and only the officer varies. No one will deny that here is the weakest point in all our polity. The British Parliaments are dissolved, not upon certain repetitions of the movements of the heavenly bodies, but according to the political exigencies with which they have to deal; a general election there marks a certain resting-place and starting-point in the fortunes of the country. But our Presidential terms regard more the tides of the ocean than those in the affairs of men. The quadrennial revolution breaks into the midst of profound peace, and takes no note of the din of arms. The late war was prolonged fifteen months on account of the presidential election of 1864, and the term of Andrew Johnson outlasts his policy even longer. These short terms cut off all opportunity of requiring a regular training of those who desire to live by conducting the details of administration, or of pensioning men of merit who give their best years to the public service; they make the politician, whether in or out of office, an adventurer; they absorb all political action and all political thought, into the single function of office-hunting; they educate a numerous class of men, otherwise useful to society, into habits of unthrift, dependence, insincerity, bad faith, and unscrupulousness; give this very class an undue influence on the public weal; intensify the heat and paralyze the thought of every canvass; make every citizen impotent, who cannot or will not spend every waking hour of his life in plotting and counterplotting; and play the ultimate control of the republic into the hands of a gang intended by nature for common gamesters, who buy and sell, not the politicians only, but the people who vote for them.

Repulsive as is this too familiar picture, it is traceable directly to the constitutional provision which makes our Presidents elective not only for stated terms, but elective by the people at large, without the intervention of any recognized representation for purposes of deliberation and nomination; or, more particularly, to the failure of the effort of the framers of the Constitution to provide a representation for that purpose in the colleges of presidential electors. Our form of government is a representative democracy for purposes of legislation; for purposes of administration, that is to say, for the purpose of electing the chief administrative functionary, it is not a representative democracy at all, but an elective monarchy, spawned of a wild attempt at a direct democracy. Thirty-five millions of people, scattered over a continent, are called upon to elect their chief magistrate by an immediate vote. The impossibility of such a thing is profoundly ignored by the law. That an election presupposes nominations, deliberations, and a repetition of the act of voting, to effect the combination of many minorities into one majority, is simply disregarded. Every voter armed with a blank slip of paper and a pencil, and posted at the aperture of a letter box, is left to construct a right of self-government out of these materials as best he may.

The first effort to do this disclosed the impossibility of concentrating a majority of votes upon a candidate, without consultation by means of some sort of a representation. Resort was had, at the outset, to the component parts of a representation provided by law for another purpose, the members of Congress, belonging to the party which desired to nominate. A caucus of Congressmen of the Republican party nominated Jefferson in 1800, Madison in 1808 and 1812, Monroe in 1816, and Crawford in 1824. But as these caucusses were composed of the members of one party only, a majority of their votes represented but a small minority of the people. Remote from their constituencies, and yet dependent on them, they neither gratified their wishes nor commanded their support. Nor was their assumption of the function of nominating candidates very generally acquiesced in. The legislatures of the larger States regarded themselves as about equally well qualified to exercise it, or, at least, to supervise its exercise. The Assembly of Virginia in particular, were considered peculiarly potent in such questions; and are said to be responsible for the choice made between Madison and Monroe as the party candidate in 1808. In 1812 the Republican legislature of New York raised up an opposition candidate in De Witt Clinton; and in 1825 Jackson was put in nomination by the legislature of Tennessee. In 1824 King Caucus broke down completely; three competing republican candidates entered the lists through legislative and other machinery, and the election went to the House, where the caucus nominee was badly worsted.

No one has ever seriously proposed to return to the caucus system, which was superseded by what, at that time, was advocated as a brilliant reform. Each party now did for itself, voluntarily, just what the law ought to have done, compulsorily, for the people. It provided itself with a systematic representation. In 1812 a voluntary convention of the opposition, attended by delegates from eleven States, was held in the city of New York, and nominated Clinton. The next national convention was that held by the Anti-Masons at Philadelphia, in 1830, at which they called a further convention of their party, of "delegates equal in number to their representatives" (meaning to the representatives of the people) "in both Houses of Congress, to make nominations," thus virtually adding a far-reaching provision to the Constitution of the United

States. The Baltimore Jackson convention of 1831, not required for the nomination of a President, and only called to fix upon a candidate for the second office, adopted this organic principle, and thus decided the fate of the country for thirty years to come. The national conventions of each party have never since failed to precede and control our presidential elections. The delegates to these gatherings were at first selected by the members of the State legislatures belonging to the respective parties. But it was logical and reasonable to say that the legitimate organ for the purpose, in each State, is a State convention of the party formed, by analogy to the national convention, of delegates corresponding to the State representatives in the State legislature. The further application of the same principle called for county conventions. And the delegates to the county conventions are now elected in " primary meetings," held in the respective wards and townships: the partisan folkmotes of the nineteenth century.

It is probable that neither county nor State conventions would ever have been heard of, if national conventions had not made a demand for them, in other words, if the President had never been made elective by the people. Once to hand, however, the State convention proved a convenient organ for nominating State officers, and the county convention was equally well adapted for the nomination of county officers. In its turn this perfection of machinery led, after 1830, to further constitutional changes. Up to that period few executive officers, except the President and the Governors had been made elective at the polls; the clumsiness of the method had been felt, and others preferred. But the hierarchy of conventions now bred a class of professional politicians who needed work to do, and emoluments to divide. The new profession, like others before it, made business for itself. It was pronounced essential to democracy to elect officers " by the people," for a stated term; and to "rotate in office," so that as many incapables as possible might be amused with hopes of a share in the plunder. As if for the express purpose of developing the system to its utmost capacity, offices were multiplied without stint. Even the clerks of the courts ceased to be creatures of the judges, and were popularly elected for stated terms. In consequence, the judges lost all power of discipline or regulation over their own official business. The official act of a ministerial officer of a court of justice is, and must be, in contemplation of law, the act of the court. But at the present day, if a judge is informed of the grossest misconduct on the part of his clerk, he can only advise the victim to indict the offender. And if the offender is clerk of the Quarter Sessions, he will be the custodian of the record of his own prosecution. As this process of multiplication continued, the "ticket" became longer than could have been given by rote, and the offices with their complicated functions and involved relations to each other, now form a puzzle which but few of the most plodding lawyers assume to unravel. Of course every idea of intelligent action in the designation of candidates, by the individual citizen, was henceforth at an end. Without politicians to enlighten him, he could not ascertain, in a year's time, what offices are to be filled at the next ensuing election; much less find persons ready and qualified to fill them. Even astute politicians have been known to waste their labors in "pipe-laying" for offices, under the mistaken impression that they were to be the subjects of the next contest at the polls.

Thus we are governed by two systems of representation; one, for purposes of legislation; the other for the selection of executive and administrative functionaries. The former is legally recognized, and stands for the whole people, not for a party of them; the representatives receive a stated compensation, and are not, in general, overworked. They are now nominated, like the executive officers, by the latter representation. It is not surprising that their power has gradually passed into the hands of those who control their official existence. The conventional representation, so to speak, has become the real source of power. It might here have been supposed, however, that the people might as well rule by the latter as by the former; and that, so far as the people are concerned, the change has been simply one of organs.

The fact is otherwise. The persons who, by means of the conventional representation, succeed in getting themselves elected, are beyond the reach of the people during their official term, and do not find it to their interest to serve them. The conventional representation is purely voluntary, is unknown to the laws, and those who conduct it are in no wise amenable to the State. Each of the two or three contemporary conventional representations stands for one party only; and partisan services are the only ones by which practical advantages are to be reaped in the service. The voluntary representatives have no prospect of compensation but such as they expect to secure from the offices to be distributed, or from the retention of those previously obtained. Competition between party and party leads to the crowding of both parties with wire-pullers, and this to a frantic scramble of the wire-pullers within the pale of each party. Intrigue permeates intrigue; and while even the most assiduous intriguer may accomplish nothing, the man who does not sacrifice everything to intrigue has not even a chance. The citizen who has a calling, an interest, a duty, or a taste outside of "politics" is powerless. The word "politics" has come to designate exclusively the manipulations of nominations and appointments. "This war is not a political war," used to be a favorite apothegm of the well-meaning of both parties. It meant that the preservation of the country ought not to be made a convenience for the distribution of patronage. This inefficiency of the citizen is not his fault, but his misfortune. For years it was the habit of party organs to upbraid "good citizens" with remissness in keeping aloof from primary meetings, and to imply that a reform in this respect would reform the body politic altogether. The advice was never acted on. It will not be seriously pretended that the mere presence of the good citizens would have had the desired effect. They would simply have swelled the number of wires to be pulled, not at all the difficulty of pulling them; to do more, they must have driven the trade of pulling themselves. The occupation is of a character to be barely tolerable under the stimulus of sport or cupidity. Patriotism, as a motive, is not sufficiently irritant in its action. You might as well expect a man, from pure love of country, to beguile his leisure hours by doing the work of a detective, a copyist, or a tax-gatherer. Indeed, there is so positive a repugnance between an interest in the merits of public measures, and an interest in the scramble of office-hunters, that the two are found united in only a very limited number of individuals, exceptionally organized.

But while the citizen is bereft of influence, it by no means follows that the politician governs. The crumbs of office have been pounded up into a mere dust, quite insufficient to support so large a flock of ravens; and the shortness of the official term prevents any feeling of security, or any habits of thrift. It is the fate of the mercenary man to be not the master but the slave of other men's money; and the wire-puller has found his patron in the capitalist, who desires to make profit out of governmental power. The professional politicians seek only power to find subjection. *Dominationis in alios servitium suum mercedem dat.*

Moneyed men associated under various titles, have gradually bought up, under the name of corporate privileges, the more important prerogatives of taxation and administration. A generation ago they approached the leading politicians as suppliants; now they hold them in pay, and use them not only to extort further immunities, but generally to control the entire machinery of the body politic. A party in Wisconsin is said, by their opponents, to have just nominated a railway King for governor. Pennsylvania, New Jersey, and New York are notoriously "owned" by railway companies; and the heads of these corporations are the only persons universally believed to have a substantial and not an imaginary hold on the reins of power.

This, again, is the natural result of circumstances. The trading politicians, irresponsible themselves, have no means of holding others to account; every corporation boasts a stable organization, servants amenable to control, and agents confident of the support of those who put them forward. Their faithful employees are rewarded by an assured compensation, or subsistence, and some provision for declining years; those who betray them are thrust into the streets, or driven to politics for a living. With these simple but potent weapons the corporations reach the will of the politicians first, and of the legislators afterwards, and make it to the interest of both to set the designs of the corporations whom the legislators are sent to restrain, above the welfare of the people by whom the legislators are trusted.

These corporations are invaluable examples by which to study at once how power is attained, and how it is forfeited. The influence of these bodies is found useless to those who are supposed to constitute them—the stockholders. As a general thing the stock of every corporation is worthless; and, under some qualifications, it may be safely asserted that the more powerful the corporation, the more worthless the stock. The stockholders have been served by their directors just as the citizens have been served by their representatives and politicians. The difference between them lies in this, that whereas the political representatives have seen the power and their profit slip into the hands of the directors, the directors have by no means surrendered anything to the politicians. And what causes the diversity? Simply the fact that the directors, themselves, like civil officers, irremovable for a stated term, can discharge any agent, officer, or employee who does not serve their purpose, while the legislators can discharge nobody. If the legislators could at will discharge the governor and administrative officers, they, and not the railway directors, would control the State. If the stockholders, instead of electing their board for a year, and then being bound to wait a year before electing another, could assemble and displace their directors at any time, they would be masters of the corporations. If the people could at any moment assemble at their respective homes and vote the politicians out of office, they would rule the State. *The power to control consists in the power to depose.* Responsibility means removability.

It is idle to talk of suppressing, or even of discouraging or controlling corporations, without first readjusting the distribution of political power. They have become the sinews of trade—and trade is now the body of social life. Ambition and administrative ability, jostled out of the management of State affairs, have come to feel that here is the real seat of power. He who controls a corporation has a share in the control of the world. Others make laws, but he dictates them; others influence elections and appointments, but he domineers over the elected and over the appointed. Others reign, but he governs. A war on corporations, at this day, would be a war on the rulers of the country The attraction of the green baize on the administrative ability of every republican country is so potent that the last two presidents of the Swiss confederation have successively retired from the head of affairs, in the one instance to govern a railway, and in the other to manage a bank.

Now what is the full import of these words? That we live in a republic? No; for the substance of power is not in the hands of elected officers. That our institutions are democratic? No; for the masses are not the directors of corporations. That we enjoy equal rights? No; for the available rights are the franchises of the innumerable corporations, and these are as diverse, as incongruous, and as arbitrary, as accident, design, and corruption can make them. Our supposed republic is transforming itself into a congeries of little oligarchies, exercising powers as motley and as ill assorted as the rights, privileges, dignities, and traditions of the German empire before its dissolution; with only this difference that the manifold *imperia in imperio* are not territorial in their boundaries, but distribute themselves over the various branches of industry pursued by the people.

Why, then, do we continue to form corporations, and to invest our money in them? Not, certainly, for the mere purpose of founding directorships for ambitious young business men. The motive for investing in corporate stock is the desire to make unlimited profits, coupled with the wish to limit the possibilities of loss. It is important to the public that an enterprise should be undertaken; but it is costly, and the chances of return are uncertain. Individuals refuse to make themselves personally responsible, because unwilling to risk their all upon it; but they are willing to stake certain definite sums, in consideration of the chances of the profits. The arrangement is regarded as mutually advantageous to the capitalists and to the public; and the State, as the representative of the public, gives its sanction. The corporators do a portion of its work, in consideration of exercising a part of its sovereignty.

But the contemplated results are not attained. Either the enterprise is not remunerative, and then the stockholders lose their money to the creditors of the corporation; or the enterprise pays, and then the stockholders lose their money to the directors; but in either case they lose their money. Who would be a stockholder? But without stockholders there can be no corporations. For many years the motive with which stocks are purchased has been once in ten times the hope of earning dividends, and nine times in ten the hope of profiting by a sale. Such a calculation is based on the assumption that the proportion of dupes to cozeners is as nine to one. But it is in the nature of such figures constantly to diminish; the advance of intelligence, when directed by cupidity, however sluggish, is steady. The conviction that shares of stock are candles lit at both ends must grow upon the public.

And if the system were calculated for immortality, and it stockholders always received their dues, would it commend itself to the approbation of the statesman? The State no longer encourages lotteries, but in many instances represses them. What is a joint stock enterprise but a lottery created for a definite industrial purpose? "The wealth acquired by speculation," says Jefferson, "is fugacious in its nature, and fills society with the spirit of gambling. The moderate and sure income of husbandry begets permanent improvement, quiet life, and orderly conduct, both public and private." The government which encourages investments in stock demoralizes, by squandering its own functions and dignities. Why, then, should it surprise us, that under such a system, politics, that is to say the State, should incur public contempt, and that the respect of the public should be diverted upon these lottery managers who succeed to the State's prerogatives? If the public interests require a risk to be run, who ought to run it? The public. And who acts for the public? The State. Who is, in the nature of things, the universal insurer? The government. If the money is lost, the State can afford to lose it. If a profit is reaped, it should swell the public coffers, and reduce taxation. Whether the money is lost or gained, the liberties of the people should remain in the keeping of the public authorities, and the control of the public enterprise should not be farmed out to private men. The State insures the individual's life, liberty, and property. It should also insure the success of all public enterprises, because they are its own. The citizen has a right to all reasonable public conveniences, whether individuals will wager money on their lucrativeness or not. He should not be governed by private men, on the plea that those private men have staked private moneys on the success of public enterprises.

Why do we cry out against this doctrine? Because we protest that administrative ability and integrity are not to be found in the organs of the State, but only in the boards of the corporations. If the case were reversed, would not our opinions follow? In the year 1866 a kingdom, not greatly favored in natural resources, successfully sustained a tremendous war without incurring a debt. Why? Because for centuries all its talent and integrity have been concentrated on its administration. Why is it otherwise here? Because our political mal-organization has elbowed ability and integrity out of our political into our corporate and private administration. We make the evil caused by our own indolence a reason for perpetuating and extending it.

Even if, wedded to inveterate theories, we are determined to leave the virtual control of our destinies in the hands of private corporations, we are at liberty to do so while readjusting our political balance in such a way as to permit capable and honest men to re-enter the political service. After accomplishing that, it will be for us to consider, whether we shall continue to restrict the functions of our statesmen to spheres out of which no one cares to make money by getting a charter, or whether the regenerate State shall resume some of the prerogatives so long relinquished.

Recapitulating, briefly, our historical summary, we contend that our institutions have, in common with the republics of ancient Greece, only the public spirit of our citizens, and with Rome, the appreciation of the necessity of basing government on fixed principles of law. From our Teutonic ancestors we derive the great foundation stone of local self-government in every vicinage, as developed through many vicissitudes, into the towns of New England, and kindred institutions of other States. To the constitutions of Charlemagne, we trace the further evolution of this general principle in the establishment of shires and counties as intermediate links between local and central authority, by means of a virtual, if not a formal representation. Ever since the days of the Norman kings of England, we have known local self-government in chartered boroughs.

Receiving these traditions from the British Isles, we have engrafted upon them what may be called the principle of integral confederation, the principle of the subordination of property to man, that of universal suffrage, and that of the emanation of government from the will of the governed. These we regard as the vital elements of our polity, none of which could be abolished without destroying its essential character. And we claim, without fear of further contradiction, that not only is it not to any one of these principles that the prevailing corruption of our politics is to be ascribed, but that, on the contrary, their tendency is adverse to it, and where preserved in or restored to their purity, they are the strongest possible safeguards against it. It was in ancient Rome, where all but two of them were wanting, that we detect more similarity to our own country in reference to this tendency to political disease, than to any other state of history. In our own country we find more political health where these leading features have been best preserved; and we find the evil to date from the very period when they began to be obscured.

Other features of our polity are the system of representation in State legislatures and in Congress as successors of the Parliament of Great Britain; the ballot; and the equalization of election districts. They are neither, we apprehend, essential to the preservation of our liberties, nor are they answerable for the results we now deplore Indirectly they may have contributed to produce the latter by occupying a disproportionate importance in the public mind, and withdrawing attention, and thereby withdrawing immediate vigor and efficacy, from those older and better institutions; and they were the occasion, if not the cause, of the gradual oblivion of the organization and totality of constituencies, and thereby of the importance of these local entities as preservatives of the life blood of healthy self-government; but these missteps might be recalled without interfering with the institutions in question; and the destruction of the latter affords no promise whatever of a reform of the ills complained of.

A third class of peculiarities consists of the direct election of other than legislative officers, and of the tenures of office for stated terms. These two usages, never asserted as principles, are certainly excrescences on our system, which not only may be discarded without impairing its essence, but which must be excoriated to preserve that essence from destruction. Eighty years ago they were applied in the designation of the chief magistrate of the republic. Forty-three years later, they had bred the National Party Convention. State and county conventions followed. Next ensued the election of all officers by the people; "the ticket, the whole ticket, and nothing but the ticket;" the multiplication of offices; the nonentity of the voter; the venality of legislators; and the supremacy of corporations. All these would be the baseless fabric of a vision, if presidents and governors were not elected by direct votes, and if offices were not held for stated terms. We submit that our promise to prove that the political corruption of the times is the result not of the essentials, but of the accidents, of our form of government, has been made good. And if we have rightly probed the evil, the cure will not be difficult; the treatment of a disease gives the physician no trouble, if he is assured of the correctness of his diagnosis. States, like animals, are not made, but grow; their very disorders are stages of their growth, and must be disarmed by assisting their restorative rather than by counteracting their destructive functions.

If the politicians have got the better of the people, the corporations have got the better of the politicians. In so doing, they have accomplished exactly what the people have now to perform. The facilities for moulding legislators to their will, now enjoyed by corporations, are the very facilities which ought to be in the hands of the people, the legitimate superiors of the legislators. The assemblymen and public servants must be made lobby agents of the people; must look to the people for funds, for direction, for preferment, for pensions, if faithful; for dismissal, if false. Coherence and consistency of authority and of responsibility must be introduced into all the relations of principal and agent, superior and inferior. Every one invested with a delegated authority, must hold office at the will of the authority appointing him; and every appointing authority, whether consisting of an individual, or of a number of individuals, must be prepared at a day's notice, to issue a fiat of revocation as unmistakable and effective as the discharge by a board of directors of any of their workmen. In a word, the problem is to *incorporate the people*. Let the people organize *as a corporation*, and thereby become the largest, the wealthiest, and the mightiest corporation in the republic.

How are the people to be incorporated? The answer is contained in what has been already said, and requires only a recapitulation here. The incorporation of the people involves a return to the method of popular self-government, the terms of which are strongly imbedded in our polity, but temporarily buried under a mass of rubbish, partly resulting from abuses, and partly produced by ill-advised reforms.

1. *Offices must cease to be held for stated terms.* This is the law not only of every well managed corporation, but of all rational private business. No sensible man, in ordinary life, would appoint his foreman for one year, and his journeymen for three years, and make each of them independent of the other, and of their employer.

2. *All subaltern executive officers must report to and hold office at the will of their immediate superiors.* This results from the same principle.

3. *Candidates for subaltern executive offices must undergo an examination, and superannuated officers must be pensioned.* The

economical argument furnished by this system against frequent and unwarranted changes, is itself of manifest value.

4. *Elections must be held at meetings of organized bodies, where deliberation may be had and nominations made, and, where it is practicable, to vote repeatedly, if a clear majority is not obtained at the first poll.* In other words, national and local nominating conventions must be abolished, and the work for which they were contrived must be done by the people in lawful assemblies, always ready to repair at a new sitting any mistake into which they may have been cozened or surprised the day before. The voter must cease to be a lay figure, and must act, in voting, as an intelligent and responsible being.

5. *The chief executive officer must report to, and must hold his office at the will of the popular body of the legislature.* This is an innovation upon our practice, but not upon that of Great Britain.

In England, at this day, the chief executive officer is not the king, but the *premier;* and the premier comes in and goes out under a vote of confidence or of non-confidence by the House of Commons. Hence, there is never a discord between the power which makes the laws and the power which executes them. Changes of ministry are, upon the whole, less frequent than Presidential campaigns are with us; but they always bring relief and never oppression. The disease breaks out and cures itself, the old cabinet goes out and the new enters, not according to the almanac, but according to the requirements of the political situation. It is otherwise, but it is not better, with us. Here the veto of the President, without giving efficacy to his own policy, may paralyze that of the people just vindicated in an animated canvass. The laws made by the legislature may become waste paper by the omission of the Executive to enforce them. The President may stultify the country by sending ministers abroad after the Senate has voted them ineligible. Congress may retort on the Executive by depriving him (like a judge of a State court) of the power of removing his own subordinates, or of filling vacancies. The President may vainly request a Secretary to resign; the subordinate may refer the request to Congress, when in session; may contemn the mandate of the commander-in-chief of the armies and navies; and may bow in submission before the "acceptance" of a general. All these things might be expunged by the same provision which would forever dispense with the necessity of national conventions.

It is true that when the king of England was removed from our system, some method had to be devised for selecting governors; and that a general election by the people appears, at first blush, the most democratic process possible. But it is a fallacy to argue that the principle of democracy *necessarily* calls for this method of designation. The most democratic administration conceivable is that which is conducted by the people themselves, in their collective capacity, in general meeting assembled. While it may be democratic for the people of a township to elect a supervisor of highways at the begining of the year, and receive his report at the close, it is more democratic still for the same people to deliberate upon the condition of their roads from week to week, and, by resolutions and votes, take those measures which the supervisor must take in their place. A large State does not admit of this sort of administration; hence the necessity of representation. But it would be none the less democratic for the people of each legislative district, in electing their assemblyman, revocable by themselves, to instruct him upon what principles, from his seat in the assembly, to influence the administration, by voting in the election or displacement of governor, by that assembly, than it is for the same people to vote in hotchpot with the body of electors of the entire State, for a governor irremovable during a fixed term of service. In practice the former course is infinitely the more democratic of the two. It avoids that primordial source of all misrule, a responsibility divided between a legislative house and an administrative functionary, neither amenable to the other. A local representative is in most cases personally known to the elector, and in some slight degree interested in courting his good-will and avoiding his displeasure. A candidate voted for over a whole State, is personally known, outside of his immediate locality, only to the busy politicians—who thus constitute a virtual aristocracy. If the State government were either administered directly by the assembly, as the affairs of the Confederation were administered by the Continental Congress, or if the governor were elected and removed at the will of the assembly, it is fair to presume that every district would send one of its better men to represent it, and that the head of the administration would be rather above than below the average of the assemblymen. At present the governor is not always so far above the average of the assemblymen as he should be, while the assemblyman is generally selected as being the most proper man to quit the country. And yet, even now, the governor is nominated, and, therefore, is virtually placed in power, by a body having the forms and the machinery of an assembly, but irresponsible and unauthorized. So indispensable is an organized deliberative body of some kind to the elevation to office of one man by many.

6. *The members of the popular body of the legislatures must hold their seats at the will of organized constituencies.* Without such a provision the legislature, empowered to appoint and remove the Executive at pleasure, would become an oligarchy. With it, their own amenability to recall would prevent the abuse of their power. There would be no discord between a member and his constituency. Any misrepresentation of the latter by the former, whether from good or evil motives, would be open to immediate correction. The majorities in the House would not fluctuate from general election to general election, but would change as gradually as public opinion changes. A new set of ideas would pervade constituency after constituency, and thus carry vote after vote in the legislature, and the majority once assured, would be as stable as it was slow in coming to a head. Leading ideas come and go, not from year to year, but from generation to generation. Hence, a man sent to the legislature in the prime of life, might well hope to remain substantially in accord with his constituents until a new growth of young men among them should supersede him with one more in unison with their younger aspirations, promoting him to some administrative position of higher dignity, though, perhaps, of less influence on legislation. In that case the legislature might come to be composed of men as well versed in affairs as are now the directors of a bank or a cotton factory.

7. *Where a constituency is too large to be assembled in a single town meeting, it must act, in seating and unseating legislators, through the instrumentality of a local popular body, similar and corresponding to the popular body of the general legislature.* In other words, the Congressmen from each State must hold their seats at the will of the State assembly, and the State assemblyman from each county in the State must hold his seat at the will of the county assembly.

For reasons already set forth, we consider the introduction of county assemblies as an innovation in name only. They have existed, in point of fact, ever since the establishment of counties themselves. The only change proposed is to make them consist of representatives elected by the respective hundreds, in town meeting, and revocable by the same authority, and to invest them with the additional function of electing, and at pleasure recalling the representative to the State assembly. The county assembly would adopt the parliamentary forms, which have approved themselves as the best method of resolving the wishes of many co-ordinate persons into a single will. They would be endowed with the freedom of action, and subjected to the accountability which representative self-government requires. The methods of the nineteenth century would be engrafted on the intentions of Charlemagne. The county assemblies would form the best of training schools for the statesmanship to be exercised in wider fields of action. This remark, however, is an adaptation to views derived from the existing state of things, which would shortly cease to be applicable, for the county assemblies would soon exceed in practical importance the State and the central government, just as the administration of a man's private affairs outweighs, in his eyes, all other affairs put together. As the confidence of the people in their home organ of legislation and administration increased, its functions would insensibly enlarge, until, at length, no subjects of deliberation would be referred to the State or the Union, but those practically incapable of treatment by the county. Thus, incidentally, the practical struggle between State rights and national sovereignty would be dissolved into its elements. Judicially, the State government should always overtop the counties, and the Federal authority should be paramount to them all, and if, in case of a rebellion or reaction in any part of the country, or to carry out a public work of transcendent magnitude, the safety, perpetuity, and prosperity of the whole should make it necessary, the higher authorities should be unembarrassed by legal technicalities in absorbing all or any of the functions of the lower. As a matter of policy, on the other hand, the people should be habituated to act as much as possible by their domestic, and as little as possible by their more distant organs; and should return to that practice after every departure from it, whenever things reverted to their normal condition.

8. *The smallest and ultimate constituency must be the hundred.* That is to say, it must number from a hundred to three hundred voters, numerous enough to find seats in the same hall, and not too numerous to deliberate without confusion; it must be so small and compact as to enable the voters to assemble without travelling away from their homes, and in the evenings of the week without prejudice to their daily avocations. These neighborhood constituencies bring the real and ultimate power of the body politic to reside, where alone the individual voter can make himself heard and felt, in the town meetings, or folkmotes, for with them lies not only the local administration but also the ultimate power of appointment of the men who form the higher governments. Nor is there any reason to fear that where the mass of voters do not rank very high in the scale of intelligence, removals and appointments would be unduly frequent. The most illiterate "boss" whose authority to discharge his workmen is unquestioned, is as little hasty in its

exercise as the best informed merchant or manufacturer. The occasion rarely presents itself, because the employee finds it to his interest to give satisfaction. For the same reason it may be confidently predicted that, under the proposed system, abrupt political changes would be of rarer occurrence than in the present constitutional monarchies of Europe. The county assemblymen would probably be composed, in nearly equal proportions, of retired or well-to-do farmers and business men, such as those from which the invaluable class of *associate judges* was, until lately, recruited in Pennsylvania; and of ambitious young professional men and ready speakers. Entirely dependent, politically, on their friends and neighbors, they could never lord it over them; and yet being necessarily chosen for parts or position, they would lead by means of these same qualities, and would exert a healthful influence over the masses. The State and Federal governments would stand upon the shoulders of such men, and the influence of the people upon the State and Federal governments would reach them after passing through the alembics formed by these well-selected local representative bodies.

9. *The local constituencies should have their executive governments organized in analogy to the executive organization here proposed for the general government.* That is to say, the governors should be elected and removed at the will of the State assemblies, the sheriffs at the will of the county assemblies, and the hundreds at the will of the folkmote.

10. *The entire State, the urban as well as the rural districts, should be divided into hundreds, compact in form, and as nearly equal as may be in population.*

11. *All the hundreds should be grouped into counties, likewise compact in form, and as nearly equal as may be in population.*

12. *An urban community embracing one or more hundreds, but less than a county, should be called a borough; and one embracing one or more counties, a city.*

13. *Where a borough is so large as to include several hundreds,* the hundreds should delegate representatives to a borough assembly or council for municipal purposes, but each hundred should act for itself in the election for delegates to the county assembly and in local self-government. The representative of the hundred in the borough council should also be the representative of the same hundred in the county assembly. By this means the hundreds, whether embraced in boroughs or not, are preserved as the fountain heads of power. The borough has a unitary municipal organization. That organization is in accord and harmony with the hundreds on the one hand

and with the county governments on the other. And the voters residing in rural hundreds, and those residing in borough hundreds, are neither privileged nor prejudiced with respect to each other.

14. *Where a city is so large as to comprise several counties*, the county assemblies of the counties composing it, should assemble as one body, forming the city council or assembly, for all purposes except that of electing representatives to the State assembly; for which purpose the members of the city assembly, coming from the respective counties, should constitute separate county colleges. By this means the city government will continue in harmony with the State government, and will fit into it as an integral component. The rural and the urban counties will neither be prejudiced nor privileged in respect of each other. The city will be a unit for municipal and administrative purposes, and there will be no incoherence between city and county organizations; the city and the hundreds will accord together as the spire with the church. The hundreds will be the foundation stone of every part of the political edifice, and the hundreds of the cities, boroughs, and country districts will stand upon the same footing.

What we now call cities are things of very recent date in this country as well as in England. Even the boroughs broke in upon the original features of the old Teutonic and feudal system, and were so small and compact as to require but a very simple organization. From what Macaulay tells us, London could not have been much of a place in the days of Charles II. Soon after the close of his reign the British government assumed the form which remained almost unchanged down to the passage of the Reform Bill of 1831. Bristol was far behind London as a town, and Liverpool, Manchester, Birmingham, Leeds, and Sheffield are the growth of the present century. London, moreover, was the seat of Parliament. By an easy transition the government of the capital became a part of the business of the senate of the empire. The routine and detail of the rude municipal institutions of London, handed down from the Middle Ages, remained with the local civic authorities, elected by the burghers. But every new municipal measure of importance was introduced by act of Parliament, and the new functions to be exercised under such innovations were not assigned to the old local functionaries, but to commissioners specially formed by the same legislation; and made dependent, not on the Lord Mayor and councils, but on the House of Commons. The anomaly was not felt as a grievance, because the men who led in Parliament were themselves residents of London, and because the citizens could always obtain the ear of Parliament where a reform was greatly needed.

As the other towns expanded their proportions, the precedents were followed which had been set in the case of London; but not with the same result. These provincial municipalities were not at all in sympathy with the House of Commons; they sprang from a different stock, and were children of another spirit. The Reform Bill was the fruit of this antipathy, more than of any other circumstance, and the spite of the landed aristocracy towards these cotton and iron lords and their supporters has just vented itself in that remarkable amendment of Lord Cairns, which practically singles out these "three cornered constituencies" for partial neutralization in the legislature, by giving one of their three representative votes to the minorities of their electors. It is highly significant that the restiveness of the large boroughs took the direction of an effort to reconstruct the Parliament of the realm, instead of a determination to vindicate the rights of local self-government. The glaring inequality of social condition between the operative masses and the leading manufacturers, wider than that which separates the country gentleman from the yeomanry, probably deterred the ironmasters from applying the principles of self-government, the pride of the landed aristocracy, to their own case, and disposed them to prefer a contest in Parliament to a partition of municipal power with their own workmen. At all events the great towns of England are practically an exception to the local self-government which is fundamental to the rest of the country, and are, really, what the current theory supposes all districts to be, mere territorial divisions administered by parliamentary authority.

With the exception, perhaps, of Bristol, none of the English provincial towns were large during the period of our colonial vassalage, in which our institutions were fashioned by English hands. No city government was constituted in New England for more than a century and a half after the first settlement, none in Massachusetts for more than two hundred years. There, in law, a city is a town, the difference between them being only in internal administration; the former managing its affairs by representatives chosen by its citizens; the latter by votes of the whole body of citizens in town meeting. In course of time, however, almost every one of the thirteen colonies had its little London, petted by its assembly as the capital of England was petted by Parliament. Boston is the only one of these metropoles which has kept the State government within her walls. When Hamilton proposed the assumption of the separate State debts on the part of the Federal government, he received the support of the moneyed States of the North, who cheerfully assumed the burden of taxation in consideration of the realization of principal and interest on these doubtful claims, and encountered the opposition of the moneyless South, who saw no prospect of compensation for the burden of increased taxation. It required all the influence of Washington to bridge the chasm. One of the inducements offered was the transfer of the seat of government to the banks of the Potomac. Had our railroads been then in operation, such a measure would have been impracticable. How different would have been the course of events, if New York or Philadelphia had remained the political capital!

Partly under the influence of this example, partly in pursuit of the rage for landed speculation which ensued at the close of the last century, and partly in consequence of the triumph of the Jeffersonian democracy, the country party, most of the States removed their governments to some small central village, between the years 1795 and 1810; and the States subsequently formed have followed the precedents. The effect has been that whereas, in England, the sense of local self-government is infinitely stronger in the country than in the large towns, it is, here, almost keener in the large towns than in the country.

If Manchester disliked to be governed by London, it was not to be expected that Philadelphia would submit to dictation at the hands of Harrisburg, or New York at those of Albany. Nor for years can such frowardness be said to have been attempted. In form, indeed, the city received its municipal organization from the State, not as the recognition of a fundamental right, but as a boon; and when an organic change was effected, it bore the stamp of an act of the State legislature. In point of fact, however, these enactments were inspired by men of consideration in the localities to be affected, and were so drawn as to confer the power of local self-government upon the inhabitants, to quite as large an extent as they were enjoyed by the people of the rural districts. The cities were made to coincide with the counties in boundary, and the county and civic organizations, though kept distinct, were in harmony, both deriving their powers from the local body of the people.

But in 1846 the mines of California came into play; "*El oro es excellentissimo*," wrote Columbus to Isabella—"it will even save souls from purgatory;" but he might have added that it will even drag nations through that venerable institution. In 1849 the baffled republicans of Europe began to immigrate; and in 1853 the railroads threw their iron meshes over the country. Thenceforth our Saturnian days were over. The large towns increased enormously, while the smaller ones dwindled away, and, in the old districts, the rural population rather diminished than increased. Business, wealth, art, literature, talent, ambition, pleasure, vice, and crime— all that concerns the influence of man upon man—were drawn into a few crowded centres. The late war brought this tendency to a climax; the great towns offered a retreat to refugees of all opinions from the debated districts, while they served as recruiting grounds for the northern army; and as centres of production for the materials of war. Even the derangement of the public finances, by making speculation rampant, and discouraging quiet industry, led to the same result. Instead of being equivalent to one county, a large city of the present day is equivalent to twenty counties. Philadelphia, once too small to people a single folkmote, could at this day man hundreds of them. Our country is as different from what it was in 1845, as it is from France or from Mexico; and it is in the large cities that the changes for better and for worse make themselves chiefly manifest.

This silent revolution offered a fair field to the lawgiver. The cities, without losing their unitary organizations, should have been divided into counties and subdivided into hundreds equivalent in population to the average of the rural counties and hundreds respectively. The city assembly, composed of a delegate from each hundred, would naturally have absorbed most of the functions of the county assemblies; and what could not be thus absorbed, ought to have been performed by the delegations representing, in the city assembly, the hundreds of each county. Even for such judicial and *quasi* judicial purposes as might and should have been left with or given to the counties, they, the counties, should have been at liberty, if desired, to perform their county functions outside of their county limits at some convenient common spot in the centre of the city. We refer to such institutions as the offices for the Recording of Deeds, those of the Register of Wills, or Surrogate, and, indeed, those of the Clerks of the Quarter Sessions and Common Pleas. Of these offices, each county, thus obtained by subdividing the city, should have its own;—a proposition from which no one will dissent who has had opportunities of comparing the facilities now afforded by such offices in the rural counties and the distressing confusion to which they are reduced in the overgrown cities. Nevertheless it might be found desirable to group into a single tier of buildings all the offices of all the counties composing the city. On no account, however, should the organization of hundreds have been omitted, as soon as a town meeting of all the citizens was found too large for orderly deliberations. For want of that, local self-government became a delusion. The idea of a democracy, in the minds of its friends and of its enemies associated itself with that of fiction; from fiction the descent is easy to deception; and deception is synonymous with fraud.

At the period which called for this reform, the national, State, and county conventions, or rather the factitious necessity which called them into being, had already operated; the evil fed upon itself, and grew by what it fed on. The illegal system of representation, resorted to for want of a better, eluded all control. Its defects were aggravated among these crowded populations. Neighbor hoodwinks neighbor with misgivings, but stranger cheats stranger with gusto. The native is fair game to the foreigner, and the foreigner to the native; the Irishman to the Dutchman and the Dutchman to the Irishman. Differences of language obstruct deliberation; differences of manners, of education, and of social position, still more. The primary meetings in large towns are now as much a dumb show as the balloting at the polls, having become, in their turn, the mere registering boards of a power behind the throne, a wheel within a wheel, which again eludes detection. The delegates to the county convention are owned by candidates or managers, and are traded off against each other, the candidate for one office agreeing for an equivalent to control "his" delegates in support of another candidate for another office. The game would be insufferably stupid, if fairly played; it derives its interest from the fact that these compacts are always broken at the decisive moment, and the final victory is to the most perfidious. At present there is hardly a pretence that the politics of a city are more than a game of fraud and chance for the spoils of office. Corruption has become so perfect that bargains and combinations are no longer confined to the politicians of the same party among themselves, but overlap the party lines and unite the managers of the opposite parties, who hold their respective followers under such excellent discipline that they can make them combat each other for the joint benefit of those who egg them on.

It is admitted on all hands that a reform is not to be accomplished by adhering to present methods. Of the remedies that have been suggested, all except the one set forth in these pages go so far as to renounce entirely the principles of universal suffrage, of democracy, of self-government. The Tories who fomented the revolution were wont to say that "this country would never be fit for gentlemen to live in, until the power of the colonial assemblies was broken." That "the country is not fit for gentlemen to live in" is a remark not rarely heard at present; and it is sometimes accompanied with the corollary that "universal suffrage won't answer," and that "we would be better off under a constitutional monarchy."

Innovations of this tendency involve a wider departure from established maxims, and are, therefore, not less but more radical than our purposed restoration of local self-government. Yet the oligarchical measures are no longer projects only; we have reached the period of a reaction against the rights of man. The ἑταιρίαι by which the aristocrats of Athens managed, at the cost of overthrowing Athens herself, to overthrow her democracy, are in action in New York and Philadelphia. A leading organ of public opinion, always sincerely in sympathy with any effort to establish equal rights in a distant quarter of the globe, has arrived at the point of saying that "the Rule of the Ring" is every year "increasing the number of sound and intelligent men, who are convinced that in a great city like New York, self-government is of necessity a standing failure." And it seriously proposes to help the matter, by substituting for that "ring" which is the product of immature local self-government, which has been reared and has been upheld by a deluded people, and is liable to be overthrown by the same power whenever informed of its interests, another "ring," which has no origin except its own lust for power, no support except the fiat of a remote State government, and no future except a coterie of office-holders, a close corporation of patricians, and their immediate dependents, or, at best, a class rule of property holders over working men. Not only has the issue between equal rights and privileges been distinctly raised, but the cause of equal rights is left, for the moment, undefended except by unthinking adhesion to existing things, including existing abuses, and by the ideas diffidently broached in these pages. To judge by the history of all ancient, mediæval, and modern cities, the ultimate results of such movements can be no other than to drive the democracy into concentrating their power into the hands of usurpers, who submerge all the efforts of oligarchical plotters in a common destruction of all political responsibility. Syracuse had her Dionysius, Geneva has her Fazy, but it would be treason to say that New York may yet have her Fernando Wood.

Far be it from us to object to the disfranchisement of the dangerous classes, so far as practicable, by any legal or moral test, which will not prejudice the innocent. Nothing could more inspire distrust of English liberalism than the opposition of such a man as Gladstone to the exclusion of convicts from the right of suffrage. We would recommend one restriction, never suggested by the advocates of a return to class rule, but likely to curb a large number who are the more anxious to direct the affairs of the nation, the more they have proved themselves incapable of managing their own; let every man be disqualified from voting, who owes a debt of record overdue. Such regulations vindicate, instead of impairing, the equality of man before the law; but every American is bound to enter his unqualified protest against the slightest tampering with the principle of universal suffrage.

The very form in which the attempt is made betrays the viciousness of its tendency, and the baselessness of its logic. Government by the governed may be very well for unsophisticated country folk, but it is a dead failure in large cities. It may be tolerated where government is almost a superfluity, but is useless where there are passions to be restrained and plots to be thwarted. We are told by a semi-official document that reform by the people of the city of New York is out of the question, because its "criminal vote" exceeds the other, by a majority of two to one. "How can you maintain self-government or universal suffrage in a community of criminals?"

In a community of criminals you cannot maintain a government of any kind; but for that very reason there never was and never will be a community of criminals. The two terms are contradictions in adjecto. Taking New York at its worst, it bears no comparison in point of criminality with the California of 1856, or the Montana of 1865, neither of which were redeemed by commissions, but both, fortunately abandoned by all the powers and principalities of the earth, were compelled to afford shining instances of the irresistible energies of local self-government.

Arguments like these reluctantly compel us to calculate the substantial extent of the evils for which such desperate measures are proposed. Our stables should not be burned; but shall we blow up a whole city to save them? After groaning our fill over the abuses of the times, we still find New York and Philadelphia safe and pleasant enough to detain us within their walls, and to attract constant accretions of men of all classes of society. We find them excellent places wherein to make and to spend money, to establish our homes, and to educate our children. Our "tax-payers" and our "better classes" say little of emigrating.

What is the practical result of the "Rule of the Ring?" The individual voter is deprived of influence on the politics of the country; the public funds are squandered; taxes are too high; criminal administration is lax; and civil justice is tedious, expensive, and not sufficiently certain. And for these evils we are asked to convert ourselves from a republic into an aristocracy, oligarchy, plutocracy, or some undefined composite of the three; to retrace the steps of our revolutionary fathers, now being wearily followed by the peoples of Europe; in order to discover, after a generation of experiment, what we are told by all history, that the individual voter is not particularly influential where the suffrage is restricted; that nowhere are the public revenues more ruthlessly drained into private purses than under the management of juntos, irresponsible to those whom they govern; that an aristocracy, once established, but above all a plutocracy, is not a whit more honest than a clique of demagogues; that, if parsimony makes a close corporation inclined to limit taxation, the same meanness leads it to hamper the industry which produces the basis of taxation; that a privileged order punishes only the crimes committed against its privileges, and itself, under the forms of law, commits crimes against the masses a thousand times more pernicious than the exploits of all the pirates of the sea; that it speedily converts justice into a prerogative of its own, which the populace must be taught to regard as something too precious for common property; that it made Europe intolerable to all but the privileged and the fortunate, until the influence of America began to tell upon it; and would destroy America because it is not what Europe was, and because it bids fair to make Europe resemble America. The teachings of Paine and Jefferson have been at times perverted and abused; they are now to be discarded. Their warnings were meant to frighten children; the generation of to-day thirsts after experience. The rebels of the South protested against the "tyranny of numbers," each of them under an indistinct impression that he would become a duke, a count, or a marquis; the reformers of the North cry out against the "criminal vote," each of them in the abiding hope that he will be made some sort of a commissioner. Southerners and Northerners are alike anxious to take good care of the people, and make them virtuous and intelligent.

Indeed, it is not intended to interfere with the political rights of the people. In politics they shall have tickets nominated for them, and shall insert those tickets into ballot boxes, with just as little difficulty, and shall shout for the successful candidates, with just as much enthusiasm, as ever. In matters of general politics the people are so well broken in, and their wings are so carefully clipped, that they can do but little harm. But politics is one thing and municipal administration another. Politics deals in nominations, elections, appointments, platforms, resolutions, commonplaces, and generalities; municipal administration is a matter of practical business. A railroad corporation holds the entire community under its iron rod, and yet restricts the right of voting for its directors to the stockholders, because they alone furnish the funds : why should not the policemen of a city government cudgel and lock up the populace, in the comforting assurance that their places depend only on the votes of the property-holders who pay the taxes which that populace earns by its labor? Give votes to the poor men of a city, and they will throw the burden of taxes upon the rich; what could be more nefarious? Disfranchise the poor, and they will be taxed by the commissions; what could be more equitable? The criminals are of course poor, because the way of the transgressor is hard; therefore the poor must not vote. The honest men are necessarily rich, for how else could they come by their money? Therefore the property-holders must be organized in commissions. It is idle to say that the rich have abundant means of influence, even under a system of universal suffrage, because experience shows that they are so indifferent to the robbery to which they are subjected, that they will not come to the polls; therefore they must be privileged. It is idle to say that the laborer is himself interested in keeping taxation, which is always in the end a taxation of labor, within bounds, because experience shows that where he votes he is equally happy under the taxation he imposes on the rich man, as the rich man is callous to the infliction; therefore both must be made attentive to their misery, and placed under moral discipline.

It would be treason to exercise political power in Philadelphia, by means of power derived from Westminster. Morally it is equal treason to control the local administration of New York by means of power derived from Albany.

Nothing, in English history, is more odious than the memory of the Star Chamber; its crime was precisely that which is now being committed by the commissioners who rule our cities by State authority. The Star Chamber was instituted because the great lords of the north of England had obtained, under the workings of the system of self-government, as then imperfectly developed, the mastery of the county governments. The commissions are directed against the politicians who, under the workings of the system of self-government as now imperfectly developed, control the politics of our cities. Where everything connected with an election, except the mechanical act of voting, is shuffling and thimble rigging, the criminal has the advantage over honest men, and may control their votes; and where, the vote once cast, the fruits of his turpitude, once acquired, are secured to him by law for a specific term of years, he has every inducement to exercise his talents. But if the honest and the dishonest were convened by law in the same room, to reason and act together, the man of smirched reputation would seek the shade, and after a struggle or two, the dangerous classes would as little overawe our political gatherings, as they now control the prayer-meeting and the lecture-room. Their victories, even if once or twice won, would be barren; for any action into which the majority would be surprised on a Monday, would admit of revocation on the Tuesday succeeding. At the last State election held in the city of New York, twenty thousand spurious votes are alleged, by the losing party, to have been cast under forged naturalization papers, or by "repeaters," who, after having fraudulently registered themselves in many districts, voted in all of them. It is manifest that, under the system here proposed, even an attempt to perpetuate any one of these twenty thousand frauds would be utterly out of the question.

The good and true men of the community, on the other hand, they, by whose toils and skill the cities are built, and fed, and clothed, and educated, would discover that they number more than a third of the community; that their interests are common and their patriotism equal. What we need is integrity, but integrity is not to be bought. To get honesty into our politics, let us keep money out. The evil fruits of our institutions are ascribable, not to the republicanism of the principle, but to the anti-republicanism of the application.

PRACTICAL DEFECTS

OF THE

EXISTING FORMS OF POLITICAL ACTION.

BY

LORIN BLODGET.
PHILADELPHIA.

PRACTICAL DEFECTS OF THE EXISTING FORMS OF POLITICAL ACTION.

CITIZENS whose attention is given to public affairs, rather than to what is known by the distinctive name of politics, have, for some years past, felt pressing on them an increasing tendency to separate the ordinary forms of political action from the usual business of the people; often from their knowledge, also, and from proper responsibility to an enlightened public opinion. They feel that they are, in practice, shut out from a free participation in the selection of men to conduct affairs; that combinations of persons having interests more narrow, limited, and personal, occupy the field, and to a certain extent exclude them from the performance of their duties and the exercise of their rights; and that in consequence of this exclusion, they know little of the mode in which the delicate and responsible duty of selecting candidates and initiating public measures is actually performed.

Attempts to surmount these difficulties, and to actually participate in these preliminary political duties, are often made, but rarely with success. It is easy to enjoin the duty, but quite another thing to discharge it in fact. Those who are not experts in this field, and not already admitted to it, find themselves repelled, decidedly, if not rudely, and find that the business in hand is conducted by persons who regard the presence of simple citizens rather as an intrusion than otherwise. And when the selections are finally made, through the usual agency of primary meetings, delegate elections, and choice by these delegates in convention, disinterested citizens are very likely to find that they are not represented in them. The choice has been dictated by strong personal interests, and in view of the largest distribution of personal advantages. The whole business has, in fact, passed from the hands of the general body of good citizens to the control of a class—a class not especially bad, or justly to be described as corrupt on the whole, but a class having extreme personal interests at stake, and acting almost exclusively in view of such interests. It is unreasonable to expect that the public interests will be well served by men whose sharp struggle for personal position has left them no time, even if they had the requisite capacity and fitness, to devote any thought to public measures. The field of local politics is, therefore, as we have said, occupied by those who are not disposed to admit men of different views and purposes to divide their power and diminish their advantages.

This is believed to be a just statement of the essential practical defect in the working of the existing forms and machinery of political action. Many persons, indeed, would represent the motives of those who manage primary meetings, and through them control nominations, in a much harsher light, and would ascribe to them an original intention to do the worst acts which we find the men so chosen at any time attempt. That they prepare the way for great corruptions and abuses is quite true, but this is a consequence of the general degradation of tone, rather than a deliberate purpose. It is entirely just to say, and really the severest thing that need be said, that through this agency all that relates to this high and delicate duty is degraded from the public to the personal level; that State legislation is falling to mere jobbery, and that small and corrupt purposes are pressing every other consideration from every part of the political field they can reach. Self-respecting citizens cannot follow where this debasing course leads, and they find themselves greatly fettered, embarrassed, and obstructed in attempting any correction of it. Admitting it to be their duty to participate in the primary forms of political action, as well as in the voting at elections, they are practically unable to perform that duty, for the reasons we have named. If they go singly to primary meetings they find few or none to help them; if they organize, at some labor, independent and non-professional assistance, they merely raise an opposing party, which is much more easily recruited than theirs, and which is certain, in the end, to outnumber them.

Altogether, these convenient and necessary organizations and sub-organizations—still convenient, and still necessary, however perverted, until they are superseded by something better—are so divested of the presence and concurrence of ordinary citizens, that almost any mischief may be done through them without our knowledge until it is past remedy.

It must be admitted that in attempting to correct these abuses we confront some peculiar difficulties. We must restore rights, now so much disused as to be scarcely known as rights, and we must at the same time restore a disposition to exercise these rights and powers which is even more out of use. A practical division of labor has been accepted, if not actually sought, in the case, and we have put this working machinery of politics away from us because we have not had the time to attend to it. So complicated and pressing are the personal duties and labors now falling to the hands of an active citizen, in professional life, or in business, that he, at least, seeks and claims exemption from everything that can be done for him by others. Public duties are becoming less and less prominent as duties in the minds of all classes, and it is thought reasonable and admissible for any man to stand aside from them who simply chooses to do so. Usually the controling reason is simply pre-occupation, but it may be anything; the merest sentiment of aversion suffices. We admit the justice of the claim to all who personally assert it, yet in the aggregate we, as well as they, pay so dearly for the admission that the severest reprehension is visited on them after it is too late to avert the specific misfortune. Men of restless and unrelaxing selfishness know their opportunity, and push their advantages without scruple. Disinterested citizens really desire to be relieved from care in political affairs, and schemers for personal advantage are only too glad to relieve them. If primary meetings are made uncomfortable, and if the final nominations present only a choice of evils, the best man named by either party being not such as the citizen is willing to vote for, it is unfortunately too easy to find in these facts reasons that seem good to the one who acts on them, against voting at all.

We have a conspicuous example of this state of affairs, with its legitimate results, in the city of New York. There the control obtained by the worst and most desperate phase of political action in a free community has become almost absolute. Every year increases the distance to which the mere citizen finds himself separated from his rightful relation to public affairs. It is impossible to break into the interested circle of managers, and the general disposition is to abandon the field, as within themselves, and to rely on extraneous aid for the most ordinary protection of persons and property. A powerful State government is fortunately within their reach, and through exceptional Commissions, and measures unknown, as they would be inadmissible, elsewhere, a fair condition of security is maintained. But suppose this State government and these unusual Commissions were not within their reach, who would answer for the turbulence and anarchy which would ensue? It is not too much to say that military power alone would have preserved peace in that city during the excitements of the last five years but for the intervention we have named, and even with it, we know that one or two signal occasions of the exercise of military authority have already been necessary. Let no one say, therefore, that this perversion of political organizations, and this abstention of citizens from the constant exercise of political duties, involves no serious dangers. Power is at all times an enormous stimulant to exertion, and though in this country its associations are less brilliant than elsewhere, it is the extreme of danger and of folly to leave it unguarded, and open to the seizure of whoever may attempt it.

This accepted division of labor is, as we have said, the first and most serious difficulty which confronts us. It has been developed by various causes, and it is chargeable as much to neglect of duty on the part of those who claim to be independent non-partisans, or to be free from especial obligations to party, as to excessive zeal and unjustifiable encroachments on the part of professional politicians. Much censure is often visited on men who are constantly prominent in political life as the representatives of the two great parties, but whatever the motives of such may be, they are subjected to a scrutiny that offers little opportunity for any dangerous encroachments. Few who attain to political prominence in the United States have proved corrupt, or have shown the reckless and desperate ambition so common in political struggles in other countries. The defects of the present system have not been invented or developed by designing men, they are simply the result of changes effected by insensible steps of departure from sound systems and correct practice.

To show this feature of the case fairly, and to do justice to the party organizations themselves, it is essential to refer briefly to the peculiar position the great political parties have in our system of government. In states governed on monarchical principles, political parties, as known to us, have really no place, and practically no existence. Dynastic factions, and extremist factions opposed to all dynasties, are abundant enough, but great divisions of the people, differing on views of public policy simply, are impossible. There may be parties in a representative body, and among the leading and more intelligent classes, but the body of the people have little or no share in such discussions. Even in England, where the nearest approach to free institutions exists, party divisions are altogether unlike ours. Under the practical working of our free system they were, however, very early developed, and they have been maintained, with singular consistency of character, to the present time. We are bound in justice to say of them, that from the beginning they have conferred the most important services in rendering factions of every sort impossible, and in subordinating the extreme views and extreme ambition of any small number to the interests and wishes of the great body, always nearly half the entire community, who represent the party. All experience of other nations proves that the great source of danger to free institutions is in the violence of factions, and in the desperate efforts of men who have personal strength enough to originate and to lead a faction. It seems, indeed, providentially ordered that with us no man is able to intrude his personal demands if the interests of the party are not served by them; and no aspirant, whatever his merits or claims, can organize a successful campaign of his own for political support before the people. The people may of their own motion rally to the support of a man they deem worthy, but they do so through the agency of party organizations.

Political parties also do a service of no small value in the thorough sifting they give to every candidate for prominent elective position; and though too much license is accorded to party organs, and much offensiveness of manner is shown, it is at least true that the work is thoroughly done. We may tolerate the unpleasant features, possibly, of this unrelenting scrutiny to which every aspirant is subjected, in view of the security it affords that men of indefeasible character will be put forward for elective office. Each party must and does restrain and control its aspirants; each must, and in practice does, set aside with a strong hand many who would perhaps be tolerated if they were not to be torn in tatters by the merciless hands of the opposition. In our long period of practical security from bad nominations, or from nominations as bad as we inevitably should have, if the party were not certain to be punished by defeat in consequence of making them, we have come to forget and overlook the danger against which we are protected. We should do full justice to the labors expended in good faith by partisan conventions in bringing out their best men, and in putting down the hundreds who struggle for the places of honor, only to be set aside because the necessities of the party imperatively demand it. No one man, nor any one section of a convention can so exercise authority, whatever the need of it, but the entire convention can, and the disappointed man submits, and is silent. The practical service is not less because the motive is equivocal; a whole convention might be personally gratified at the nomination of a man admitted to be bad, but the great stake of success cannot be attained under such a leader, and the virtue must be affected, whether any one of the parties to the proceeding has relish for it or not. In fact, nothing is so searching and severe upon errors and defects as this pressure of party necessity, a pressure brought to bear upon each specific case almost equally by each party; and as we have said, no faction has yet proved powerful enough in this country to face this trial in the field of national politics. No general purpose of corrupt legislation has ever succeeded under it, and, we believe, none ever can.

And quite as striking as the annihilation of abuses of this more positive sort, has been the extinction of weak attempts to mislead the people into new parties, and to substitute small and specious compromises for vital principles. No man, however great his temporary power, can accomplish such ends in the face of party organizations; nor can any set of men, misled into the belief that they can erect a new standard without the public concurrence, survive a trial of strength with the great parties founded on the convictions, or even on the real prejudices, of the people at large. In the haste of passing events we forget how many attempts of this sort have been made within a brief period of years, and how signal the lesson has been to those who have wrecked themselves in the inevitable failures.

This may at first appear to be a mere rehearsal of platitudes as to the agency and nature of political parties, but its pertinence is seen when we undertake to provide any substitutes for, or modifications of, these parties. If we are not to get anything better, and find no need to modify them in their greater relations, we must see to their maintenance, either by the aid of the machinery we have, or by some other agencies. They certainly involve great labor, and an extensive if not complicated detail of organization and sub-organization. This is more necessary also when operations are conducted over a large territory; there must be communication and coherence; there must be practical interests in common, and an actual realization of benefits to those who constitute the working machinery. It is often thought that no party can be pure in which political rewards are relied on to insure activity, but it is a short answer to this suggestion, that however desirable it may be to find persons disinterested enough to give their time and energies to the public service without reward, none have yet offered to do so, and few probably ever will. If we were to assume that a great party should repel all whose activity was inspired by hope of office or position, every practical man knows that such a party could never hope to attain to power, however just its views of public policy. In short, a great party must attach and retain to itself all men actuated by reasonably correct motives; it must make the political positions in its gift one of the incentives to its support, and it must pay for the labor necessary to maintain its organization and conduct its campaigns. Bearing in mind the fact that great numbers leave the diffusion of information on public affairs entirely to these organizations, and trust to them to inform thousands who will not inform themselves, and to bring out the reluctant, the busy and the preoccupied at all general elections, it is inevitable that severe manual labor is required, and this labor must be paid with money. Therefore parties collect and expend considerable sums on general elections, never as British aspirants for parliamentary position do, by paying each voter £5 or £10 sterling for his vote, but legitimately and properly, on the whole. In view of the bad examples set in the elections of European nations, and of the chances for mischief arising in the use of money, it is surprising how unexceptionable the working side of our political parties continues to be. And more, no class of citizens, prominent or humble, can give, without consideration, any large share of their time to the service of the public. A party must, therefore, make service in its ranks at least one of the reasons for choosing persons to occupy positions in its gift when successful. Whatever the liability of this principle to abuse, and the consequent necessity to guard against abuses, the point here made is that the fact and the practice must be accepted as a necessity, unavoidable as things are, and as they are likely to remain for an indefinite time.

We reassert these positions in summary form, to show the indispensable character of much of this machinery, namely, that great political parties are necessary in free governments; that by elevating the political field above the accidents and incidents of merely personal management, they save us from factions, and from corruption on a national scale; and that they promptly set aside the most labored shams of weak statesmanship. They cannot exist without organization, and the employment of extensive machinery; and to secure the proper activity, and the close attention of capable and effective men, they must give what may lie in their power to give, of office and personal advantage to those who devote time and attention to the actual work required.

This is the case as it appears from the point of view of a practical man, and an actual participant in affairs as they are. At the outset we gave a view taken from an outside point, such views as any intelligent citizen, practically withdrawn from the actual work, would deem both just and complete. The errors of the present situation then become very conspicuous, and it is not apparent by what steps of plausible pretext, at least, if not of inevitable necessity, we have come to such a result. It is only just, however, to show that organization, machinery, interested agents, and properly compensated labor are all inevitable; and if the possession of power gives opportunity to choose without detriment to the public interests, it would require more than human forbearance to choose an antagonist in place of a self-sacrificing friend.

But the anxiety of many to get rid of party contests may justify a word illustrating their wishes. They would greatly like to mitigate the severity of party contests, and yet most persons act as if the shortest and best road to this end is simply to get the party opposed to their views out of the way. This is, indeed, the only way—the difficulty being to persuade the said opposing party to submit to annihilation. They would, also, be glad to see party bonds released, and greater liberty for the citizen to think and act for himself. The answer is, that this personal liberty is desirable and meritorious, except when a crisis comes requiring a full vote, and absolute unanimity in the party. Then it becomes an offence, and a grave and serious offence. No single man, or handful of men, can have a right to sacrifice the welfare of the nation to gratify some impracticable personal views. It must suffice them to urge the adoption of their views on their political associates, but if not adopted, their right of dissent at a great election ends. This last is, in truth, the law of the case as it should be enforced, and as it is enforced. We not only cannot get rid of party organizations, but having perfected them to the best of our ability we demand, with the utmost earnestness and energy, that all shall conform to our party who do not conform to the side opposed to us.

This demand for unanimity of action on great occasions has been called by some severe names, and it is often repudiated as a kind of drill and discipline which is inconsistent with the proper freedom of individual opinion. Often it may be such, but in the greater number of cases the highest duty of the citizen is to conform to the line of action pointed out by the party, and his best interests are served by doing so. Very serious injuries to great measures of public policy have more than once been inflicted through personal dislike of candidates, and through resistance to small partisan abuses being carried too far. When great principles are at stake the punishment of individuals must be deferred. The people do know and feel keenly a lapse in the tone of a patriotic party caused by defeat: they are sharp to observe events on the greatest scale, and they resent incapacity as they do treachery. Indeed, the analogies of a military campaign almost precisely apply to political duties after the forces are marshalled and the leaders are in the field; we want no grumbling or personal dissent by which the battle may be lost.

Believing, as the writer does, that a party made up of men generally hostile to progress exists, and always will exist, a party of negation and obstruction, always ready to seize power through the unintelligent numbers it can control. We must insist that no time has yet come when organization and effort can be relaxed on the better side. This dead weight that an advancing state carries, this mass of reactionists, appears to be as constant, if not always as great, in its power, as the party of advancement. Its uses are now inscrutable to us, though we must not doubt that in the deeper economy of the laws of human government reasons may be found. It is the analogue in politics of the principle of evil in morals, striking as staggering and unexpected blows as that does, through agents that are clearly passive, if not involuntary. The results of some elections are as palpably disastrous as a visitation of an earthquake or a plague—an epidemic of defalcation, or a financial panic is trivial in comparison with the great chill brought on the country through a temporary triumph of the reactionists. We have much to endure in the risks of the spring elections, and if the State of Connecticut, as the most conspicuous offender, could hereafter be restrained by positive law from voting when the rest of the country is at peace, every right-minded citizen would feel relieved. Next the August and October elections come with their menace of disaster, and if the turn of affairs is to the reactionist side on these occasions, there is, almost certainly, panic and wreck in November. The national pulse is, in fact, a unit, and the public nerves centre in one head. Calamity in detail is calamity to the whole. A whole people are prostrated because of intrigues in some small nominating convention, through which intrigues two or three unworthy men get on a ticket and blacken it. Five hundred or a thousand voters revolt at this, and resolve to punish it, but in so doing they place the reactionist party in power in the early election in the East, or, still worse, in the October election in Pennsylvania, and so they let in the tide of hostility which the best of public measures always evokes, and sweep away the beneficent work of years. Clearly there are considerations that should impel us to maintain political organizations other than the personal merits or demerits of any one man who may come before us for our suffrages.

The actual working machinery of political organizations was originally and carefully framed to represent the party in good faith. It misrepresents the aggregate of the adherents of any party now only because it represents the sharp, the active and successful among those who participate in wielding it. We have in local use at Philadelphia a fair exemplification of it; first a committee of superintendence, charged with the general management, and particularly with the establishment of "Rules" by which it is everywhere to be governed. These rules prescribe with great care and particularity the entire course of proceeding, and rules which are not "fair" and just—to the participants, be it observed—could not stand a day. Under these the members of the party are invited to meet in the several precincts, at a time sufficiently in advance of any general election: first, to choose officers for conducting delegate elections; next, to elect delegates for a convention representing each of the general tickets, city, State, judicial, etc., at which conventions all candidates are placed in nomination. To these meetings and elections only those known to be adherents of the party which authorizes them are admitted, and when the candidates are selected the work of chief importance is done. The advocacy of the ticket is of course essential, and to be successful it must be conducted by the same organization. The essential feature of these proceedings is, as we have said, their strictly representative character; through delegates duly elected by a majority of votes. At each sub-election there are sub-parties also, contesting sharply for success, but in most cases yielding when defeated, and accepting a result at a precinct, with law-abiding patience, as a defeated party does an adverse Presidential election. Of course the delegate elect is bound to his ticket and his candidate by bonds which few ever attempt to break, and which it might be bad policy to advise should ever be broken. The delegates are therefore fixed in their position when they convene, and can only support the man they were chosen to support so long as he stands any chance of success. Much as we may desire that they shall exercise a wise and free discretion, it is dangerous to open the door too widely, since if the purchase of an entire legislative majority is as easy as has been reported of the greatest State in the Union, it might be possible to purchase a ward nomination, or even a number in a city delegate convention large enough to decide between evenly balanced parties supporting rival candidates for the sheriffalty, if all the delegates were elected unpledged.

We must admit that, as a rule, the several proceedings are fairly conducted; that the defeated local parties submit to the majority; that the delegates adhere to the pledges and commitments under which they were elected. The ultimate choice is, in a great majority of cases, the real choice of the majority of *participants* from the beginning to the end of the entire work of making nominations; and we again revert to the central difficulty of the case, which is the smallness of the numbers participating, and the absence of intelligent and disinterested judges of fitness for public position. Such find themselves, very naturally, quite unrepresented in many cases. The standard of the delegates was not their standard; the local and personal advantages which incited the greatest activity, and which most influenced the decision, are unknown to them. As to the numbers participating, of course from one party only, it is fair to assume that of all who are qualified as voters, little more than one-half vote at unimportant general elections, and not more than one-half of these, or one-fourth of the whole body of adherents of a party, participate in primary elections. Really, three or four shrewd and active men of each precinct can do what they please in obtaining a majority of the twenty or thirty who vote at that precinct at the critical primary election. If any citizen would experiment upon the facility of organizing an opposition to some aspirant of doubtful character, already in the field, he may, after great effort, get fifteen or twenty votes at the utmost, and see his distinctive ticket fail after all. The best that can usually be done is to choose wisely between names already presented, and to influence others as much and as favorably as possible without assuming an attitude of hostility which puts an end to influence. It is, however, the least justifiable of all courses, to make this unsatisfactory character of the primary meetings a reason for abandoning all political duties; and it is equally unjustifiable to refuse to vote because the candidates may not be all they should be—of course excepting the intolerably bad.

It is also noticeable that this detail of rules causes the work done under them to recede further from us with each year. With increasing population, increasing wealth, and the attendant desires of preoccupied men to put off to the care of others everything not absolutely essential be done personally, the business strides away from us through the very means intended to secure exact representation. A ward meeting of a thousand persons convened fairly from every class in society, would represent the public sentiments and personal wishes of the people in a high degree; it would be deficient in nothing; energy, unselfishness, courage, and patriotism would be seen and felt. No unsound man would dare to face its scrutiny, or expect that a majority so convened would choose him before better men. This is the true form of the primary meeting, in fact, and the present necessity clearly is to substitute, at least for a short time, the large and full public meeting, drawn from and embracing all classes, for the detailed representative mode now in use.

The vital question is how shall a fresh departure be taken in this exercise of a great right and a great duty? How shall the inactive and neglectful be brought freshly and willingly forward? How shall the advanced and advancing tone of general public opinion be felt and seen in the conduct of our affairs? The public tone is advancing and not retrograding. Patriotic, capable and unselfish men are abundant. Why, even the legislative bribery attempted by wholesale in an adjoining State proved unsuccessful, and several of its most conspicuous agents have been laid aside by the people. And, to assert the extremest case of right crushed under existing wrong, were the people in open convention to nominate and elect officers for that purpose, the gigantic national debauchery of the whiskey tax would cease, and the money be rigidly collected. We cite these existing degradations only to deny and repudiate them as indices of public demoralization.

Much of our embarrassment, and of the apparent want of executive power to repress abuses, arises from the fact that the whole tone and text of our laws is permissive rather than mandatory. In the beginning we thought liberty the only thing needful. Permission to vote was quite enough; no patriot of revolutionary times dreamed of an age in which voluntary abstention from the exercise of such powers would become a serious evil. In accordance with this permissive general tone, we tolerate many things that ought to be regarded as intolerable. We are passive to a fault; we trust to Providence to deliver us, when it is most clearly ordered that delivery can come only from our own labors. We stand aside when a schemer pushes us at the polling places, and if the manner of a man is disagreeable, we yield him the precedence which he hoped to obtain by making himself disagreeable. Rather than go to the polls and be elbowed by a crowd, we submit to the election of men who help themselves by millions to the property of citizens —ourselves being victims, as well as those who cannot guard themselves. Nothing is so striking to a stranger as this want of care for the conduct of affairs. It is unknown elsewhere. Even in the days of confederate ascendency at the South, the incipient as well as the developed period, there were no passive ones among those qualified to lead or to participate. Part of the great delusion on which the rebellion rested was to undervalue the loyal section because of its passiveness and its supposed inability to represent its interests. It seemed reasonable to expect that we would tolerate secession, having tolerated so much and having submitted so tamely to all sorts of humiliations. We might be well enough commercially, and be very successful in trades, professions or business pursuits, but we had, they thought, neither taste nor capacity for politics. This proved to them a most costly, but it certainly was a very plausible delusion.

Our political system, in all its parts, is immovably attached to the voluntary principle, and no amendment or essential change of this is possible. Elections may be provided and ordered by law, but no citizen is bound by statute to attend them. If we can throw the authority of law about one more act, the primary meetings of the people, we shall exhaust the power of statutory regulation, and to do this proposed act will require great delicacy and skill. The entire system calls for constant exertion to educate, to inform, and to incite to the proper discharge of political duties. In the absence of the despotic element, we forget how great the prizes of power are, and how great are the efforts that desperate men feel warranted in making to obtain power. The very proper disregard of political honors which exists, is changing insensibly into a sentiment in part of contempt for such positions, and in part of abnegation of duties connected with them. This originates chiefly in the great personal successes our free institutions enable an active man to attain. Having nothing to do but to work for himself, being clogged by no disabilities, and oppressed by no exactions, a man of energy is easily successful, and being successful forgets his obligations to the State. This very liberty, and the personal triumphs achieved through it, should be credited alone to the institutions which require the aid of all right-minded men to secure their direction at the hands of competent and honorable men. If we neglect, degrade and abandon them, we have, already, ample experience of the facility with which they will fall into corrupt hands, and the lapse of duty is certain to be severely punished.

In proposing to attain one essential point of reform, that of bringing the largest possible numbers into participation in the primary meetings of the people, we find the division of parties very difficult to provide for. The law has never yet recognized the existence of parties, and it would be difficult to frame a statute providing for the declaration of a vote for candidates. As candidates they may be supported or opposed by their own party to the last moment; no choice at a primary meeting insures even their continuance in the field to be voted for. An entirely new man has rights equal to any one previously named. The law could only open the polls, perhaps, and accept votes at the hands of the proper officers, to declare nominations. But as these declarations have no final validity, the law cannot take cognizance of them. Persons so chosen would not necessarily be candidates in any authoritative sense, since a new man could with equal legality be finally elected to office. Again, the action of officers could not, consistently with the usual tenor of official duty, be made compulsory—the obligation could only exist to do an act having binding force when done. The expense and labor of a double election would also be involved, so that, altogether, it would appear inadmissible to provide that primary meetings for the election of delegates, or for direct voting to make nominations, shall be held under such regulations of law as now apply to elections themselves. Party distinctions first intervene to make the case difficult; and next, legal invalidity would attach to the result, whatever it might be, or if not so, the occasion would rise to an election; a duplicate, in labor and anxiety, of the regular election.

The preferable alternative is, as we have said, to attempt a new and more emphatic form of primary action, by voluntary organizations. The end first to be attained is to bring out the requisite numbers to participate, numbers so great as to overrule the narrow, local, and merely selfish purposes of those who make a business of politics. It is possible that the most effective step would be to enlarge the precinct meetings to ward meetings, and to elect delegates to nominating conventions by general vote of the ward. Smaller subdivisions than the ward have no distinct interests, and they are recognized in voting only for the convenience of citizens. General meetings of residents of a precinct only are scarcely practicable, yet it may be found that they can be employed, and that to do so would avert any feeling of opposition arising from an idea that the power of the people is restricted by removing the precinct selection to the ward meeting.

The case is really involved in great difficulty in consequence of the present minute official divisions recognized by law, divisions in which it is already arranged that the representative principle shall be faithfully carried out. And to do these organizations justice it must be admitted that general good faith, and a fair share of public spirit pervade their meetings. Public duties even of this sort, are often onerous, and the zeal with which they are discharged is often praiseworthy. In judging them fairly we cannot reasonably exaggerate even the hope and expectation of office into unrelieved corruption. It is more the absence of high motives, than the presence of positively bad ones, that characterizes them. It is not in the nature of things that men should devote themselves to the interests of others, or of the general public, which is much the same, without hope of remuneration or reward. Few have the time to do the actual work of attending political meetings, and in view of the inevitable contact there with the rough side of the people, large and increasing numbers are content to let others do the work, to hand it over to those whose tastes incline to it, and to complain very little whether it is well or ill done. After a few experiments at modifying and moulding these proceedings, it has been freely declared, that, on the whole, local politics are taken care of at a reasonably cheap rate by those who now devote their time to them;

the small jobbery at the command of local offices being thrown into the bargain. Citizens of the more sensitive class, whose time is valuable, could not afford to do the work for rewards so small and uncertain.

We cite these self-justifying comments of men who have tried to comply with the frequent injunctions to attend primary meetings only to illustrate the case, not to concur in them.

The existing system of voluntary organization, perfect as it is in theory, fails in practice because it fails to draw within its working circle a number of citizens sufficiently large to elevate its character and protect it from abuses. We have not thought the discussion here made of various phases and aspects of the case uncalled for, since however clearly any specific proposition of reform may be justified to the mind of one who thoroughly examines the whole ground, it is still necessary to convince many more in order to succeed in establishing any new order of things. The people must generally approve, and practically accept, any measure to make it effective. The simplest form of legal recognition of the representative system would occur to many as the readiest mode of attempting legal aid at all, but great, if not insuperable, difficulties present themselves in attempting to apply legal forms to acts which have no binding validity when performed. If the law recognizes the act, both parties must hold their primary meetings at the same time and place. If delegates are to be elected to meet in subsequent conventions and nominate, we should be little better off than now; no better off, probably, since the small addition secured to the aggregate vote would probably not change the result. But if a modification so important is made as to require these primary meetings to vote directly for candidates to be ultimately elected, this preliminary voting constituting the nomination, and showing the strength of each man with the people, it is clear that an important service would be conferred. This change would, however, involve a considerable departure from existing usages. It might also create confusion by leaving the candidacy still undefined, a second or third man, having a considerable popular vote, would still insist on going before the people, regardless of the interests of the party to which he was attached. That this might prove a grave error is very probable, since all experience proves the danger of factions, even if organized for the support of a man of quite superior character. The personal element would be more largely intruded than it now is, and facing a compact, powerful, and blind negative mass as we constantly must in the party of reaction, we cannot afford to divide over small issues, and be ruined by such division.

The practical point most easily tried is such a change in the voluntary system as will, at least for a time, bring fresh men and fresh influences to bear upon the existing machinery. It is claimed that this may most signally be done by the adoption of what is known as the Crawford County system—the selection of candidates by direct vote, instead of by delegate conventions. City or municipal divisions of territory will unquestionably render this less easy here than in the country—if the precinct divisions are maintained, the departure will be too little marked and the lapse too easy to the present inattention and small vote. If ward divisions are attempted the practical difficulty of working such larger meetings or polling places may defeat the object or incite hostility.

It is proper, in conclusion, to say, that the writer of this paper is keenly conscious of his inability to suggest a complete and adequate measure of reform in the practical working of the existing forms of political action. Many years of close observation have shown the defects of these forms in a strong light, but have indicated no other or better reliance than on the elevation and advancement of the people as a whole. The purpose of this essay has been to analyze the subject, and to suggest considerations relating to it, rather than to present any positive plan of action apart from the existing one. It is not the writer's purpose to assume that legal organization is practicable, or to decide that it is impracticable. The chief object he has is to awaken fresh attention to the duties, the powers and responsibilities of the citizen, and to make an effort to arrest the increasing separation of citizens from the whole field of political duty. Every one must feel that a great error exists on this point, and that it is making rapid progress; that the best citizens are being withdrawn from personal participation in political affairs—voluntarily with some, and against their will with others; and that this course of events is likely, at no remote day, to bring in its train far more important and more disastrous consequences than have yet appeared.

Printed in Dunstable, United Kingdom